PUTTING ON
A PLAY

by

Michael Legat

ROBERT HALE · LONDON

To
Heather

© *Rosmic Productions Ltd 1984*
First published in Great Britain 1984

ISBN 0 7090 1738 3

Robert Hale Limited
Clerkenwell House
Clerkenwell Green
London EC1R oHT

Photoset in Sabon by
Kelly Typesetting Limited
Bradford-on-Avon, Wiltshire
Printed in Great Britain by
Redwood Burn Limited
Trowbridge, Wiltshire
Bound by W.B.C. Bookbinders Limited

Contents

Foreword

It gives me tremendous pleasure to write the Foreword to Michael Legat's excellent book. I agree with so much that he says, and the no-nonsense way in which he says it. I know of few books that deal with the subject so completely, from the organizing of an Amateur Dramatic Society to the 'After the Show' Party and the much less glamorous cleaning up. And it is written in a commonsense, wise and witty way, too.

Ellen Terry once said, 'Only a great actor finds the difficulties of the actor's art infinite'—a sentiment many people working in amateur theatre would do well to reflect on. There is nothing so terrible as the arrogance of the bad amateur actor, doomed to remain forever bad, convinced that he or she can learn from no one—director, fellow actors, audience or adjudicator. How I wish such an individual could be persuaded to read this book, for there is so much to gain from it.

Directors, too, will find expert and skilful guidance here. How often have I, as adjudicator, seen promising casts floundering without the benefit of good direction, or indeed of *any* direction. Mr Legat's approach is resourceful, creative and above all *practical*. He deals with the many directorial pitfalls in a sensible and imaginative manner, but what is even more important, he never allows us to forget that the director is dealing with human beings, and the emphasis throughout is on teamwork, an aspect of the subject not much in evidence in the amateur movement.

The author is acutely conscious that effective theatre is total communication and awareness between actors and audience. To achieve this we have to find a way of successfully dealing with people and all the attendant problems they bring with them to rehearsal. This book, throughout which understanding and, indeed, compassion are always evident, will help you towards that goal.

In his Introduction Mr Legat says the book is intended for the inexperienced amateur. He is too modest. Wherever you think you are in amateur drama, and whatever level you have reached, I am positive that you will find something to interest and inform you here.

ROY SEAMMEN, LGSM
Member of the Guild of Drama Adjudicators

Introduction

Why write yet another book about amateur drama? Principally because so many of those already published seem to assume that their readers belong to large groups, act on stages which are both spacious and lavishly equipped, and rehearse in conditions which sadly have been rarely available to the amateur companies that I have known. *Putting on a Play* will, I hope, cater for small groups, new societies, and for underprivileged and inexperienced amateurs.

It does not claim to be comprehensive, and while it attempts to give some hints in such specialized fields as lighting, costume, make-up and scenery, the reader should not neglect the many excellent books which treat those subjects in depth. A large proportion of the book is devoted to direction, rehearsals and acting, and here I have tried to distil over forty years' experience in amateur drama in a helpful and practical way.

I have used masculine terms and pronouns almost exclusively in order to avoid the repeated clumsiness of 'he or she', 'himself or herself' and similar phrases. I mean no slight on the ladies—how could I, when they form the majority among those who practise amateur drama? Please accept an apology and read in the alternatives whenever appropriate.

I should like to thank the various amateur groups I have worked with over the years, and especially the S. Philip's Players, Norbury, for all the pleasure and the wide variety of experience that I have gained from them. Warm tributes are also due to my first mentor, Joan Taylor, to Teddy Ross Gower, whose direction I always enjoyed, to Kay Ross Gower, with whom it was such a joy to act, and to my wife, who forgives my constant absence at rehearsals. I am also extremely grateful to the numerous adjudicators who have taught me most of what I know about the craft of amateur drama and who have thereby provided so much of the material in this book.

M.L.

I

Organizing an Amateur Dramatic Society

Amateur drama is alive and well, living in hundreds of villages and country towns, in the suburbs and centres of great cities. It must be admitted that its health varies from time to time—some societies flourish and then fade, their membership and audiences dwindling—but it survives and provides innumerable people with a rewarding spare-time occupation.

Some enthusiasts are 'naturals', born with an instinctive sense of theatre; they know everything that this book sets out to teach, and more. Most of us, however, have to learn the craft, and once bitten by the bug spend a large part of our lives trying to build on our early experience of acting (or direction, stage design, make-up or whatever aspect of amateur drama we are involved in) so that we can achieve what the 'naturals' do without effort. But the craft *can* be learnt, and even those who at first seem to their colleagues, their audiences and themselves to be quite hopeless may turn in time into more than competent actors (or directors, designers, make-up artists or whatever).

Although you may want to concentrate on one particular branch of amateur drama, the more you know about the whole business the better, and for a start it is worthwhile to look at the way a society is organized.

The Executive Committee

Some amateur groups seem to survive and thrive with very little formal organization, usually when led by an indefatigable mortal who single-handed chooses, casts and directs the play, arranges the lighting, scenery, furniture, costumes, properties—and probably plays the leading role too. Most groups, however, prefer to distribute the work, and this usually results in the formation of a committee, with a Chairman, Secretary, Treasurer and as many other members as necessary. In general, the smaller the committee the better, provided that its members are all willing to devote whatever time is needed to the society, but it is important to see that all aspects of the group's work are adequately represented, and if, for instance, there is a youth section in your society, to have someone on the committee who will speak for the youngsters. Some companies are lucky enough to have a permanent Stage Director, Lighting Director and Wardrobe Mistress, all of whom should be members of the executive committee. The great advantage of keeping the same people in these jobs, incidentally, is that they usually know what equipment they have and will take responsibility for looking after it properly. If the director of a play is not a member of the executive committee, he should be co-opted on to it for the duration of the production.

The committee will of course carry out the usual functions. The Secretary will keep minutes and correspondence, the Treasurer will keep accounts, the Chairman will keep the peace, and the committee members will keep on talking. The committee may deal solely with the group's business and policy affairs, but more often and rightly is much concerned in the society's main interest—the putting on of plays—and is frequently in effect a production committee. This necessarily involves the members in a considerable amount of detail, and my own preference would be to form a separate production team, whose decisions can be reported back to the main committee.

Policy

If you are starting an amateur society, it is important to establish from the outset what your policy is to be: how many productions there will be each year; whether they will be full-length plays or one-acters, or a mixture; whether the society will enter festivals, and if so how often and with what kind of plays; whether you will run social functions and other activities such as lectures on various aspects of stagecraft, and if so how often; what will be done about recruitment. The answer to many of these questions must depend on the kind of people you have in your group, and your potential audience. Any new committee must give special weight to the capabilities of the members—it will be very difficult to run a programme of several productions a year with a small membership or with one that you know has many other interests.

The important thing, if you are just beginning, is to lay down your principles, including that of finance, from the very start. Before long they will be enshrined as the way the group works, and no one will grumble any more.

Finance

You will have to decide what to do about the society's funds. How will you raise money, and will the group retain any profits on its productions or will they all have to be given to a charity? Church groups often find themselves in difficulties because they hand over all profits to their church and then have no money with which to carry on, bearing in mind that it may easily cost a substantial three-figure sum to put on a full-length play. Any society should always keep a reasonable contingency fund.

Most amateur groups like to keep their membership sub-scription as low as possible, relying on the sale of tickets for their productions to make a profit and provide their income. This means that the average member of a society gets the benefits of it for very little cost. That is fine if your productions do better than break even and if your coffers are full, but many groups find it a constant struggle to keep their bank balance in the black.

How do you raise extra cash without putting subscriptions up to an unacceptable level? Some societies feel that it is fair to squeeze a little more out of those members who are cast in a play, on the grounds that they get the most fun. They ask the actors to pay for their copies of the play, which they may then keep, instead of the society buying the scripts, in which case they are returned after the production and stored—but for what purpose? Possibly to hire to another local company, but generally simply to moulder away in someone's attic. They also collect a token sum from each player at each rehearsal, a method which does not raise very much money, any more than the minuscule profit which can be made on selling coffee at rehearsals does—but every little helps. A company I know which uses this rehearsal payment system sometimes increases the fee when putting on a period play with a big bill for costumes. Most of the actors find it fairly painless.

You can also charge for other activities, such as lectures and demonstrations, playreadings, parties, and pitch the cost of entrance high enough to make a profit. Raffles and jumble sales make money. Small additional sums can be raised from families and friends of members who will pay an annual subscription to become Patrons or Friends of the society, but you need to give them something in return—copies of newsletters, priority booking of tickets, freedom to attend other functions of the group—and it sometimes becomes at best a break-even exercise.

One of the best ways of saving money is to own your own equipment—curtains, flats, lights, dimmer boards, tape recorder, costumes—so that you do not have to hire. You will need storage space, of course. If you want to buy equipment and do not have the funds available, it may be worth trying to raise interest-free loans from your members.

If your group is successful and retains its profits, it will probably be possible to provide free copies of plays for the actors and to pay all other expenses, large and small; you may even raise enough money to build or buy a club-house or your own theatre; at a less grand level you might at least be able to hire adequate rehearsal premises. If, however, you are not in that sort of position and have to ask your members to contribute financially, you sometimes meet the argument, 'We are already giving up our time, not to mention our talents—that is enough.' The answer is of course that it isn't enough. Those who take part in amateur drama get a great deal of pleasure out of it, and as with most other hobbies that we enjoy, we should not expect to get it for nothing.

Constitution

It is worth drawing up a Constitution to cover such matters as: the name of the society, its aims and objects, the conditions of membership (who is eligible to join, whether an annual subscription is payable, etc), the composition and powers of the committee and the rules for election of its members, the timing of the Annual General Meeting, the disposal of the society's funds and possessions in the event of dissolution, the arrangements for changing the Constitution and calling Extraordinary General Meetings, and so on. The use of profits made by the society may also be included, and if you have a tame accountant available it is worth contacting him to make sure that your moneys will not be liable to tax.

Annual General Meeting

You will need to hold an Annual General Meeting at which you review the past year, consider the accounts, elect your officials and committee, discuss your programme for the year ahead, and cover any other necessary business. It is a fact of life that the AGM of an amateur drama group is normally attended by a very small proportion of the membership. One company with which I have been connected has solved this problem by arranging its AGM to coincide with the audition for the Spring production. This has the desirable effect both of bringing members along and of keeping the AGM short.

The Production Committee

If, as suggested earlier, you form a special Production Committee or team, who should be on it? Ideally, I should like to see at least twelve people, as follows:

The Director. I use this term rather than 'the Producer', a title I prefer to give to the third person on my list (see below). The Director is in overall charge of the production.

The Stage Manager. In effect the Assistant Director.

The Producer. I use this term in the sense that it is used in the film business—the person who procures the materials which the director moulds into a production. He is the liaison officer between the director and all the following:

The Set Designer.

The Stage Director.

The person in charge of furniture and the dressing of the stage.

The person in charge of properties.
The Lighting Director.
The Sound Director.
The Wardrobe Mistress.
The Publicity Manager.
The Front of House Manager.

You may also wish to add the society's Treasurer to the Production Committee. At the very least a budget should be drawn up for every production, approved by the executive committee and lodged with the Treasurer. This means of course that the heads of the various departments will need to know what they already have in stock and what they will need to buy or hire. No one should spend money which is not allowed for in this budget without permission from the executive committee, and all bills and receipts should be passed promptly to the Treasurer. The estimated return from ticket sales will of course be included in the budget.

The functions of the officials listed above will be discussed in later chapters. It is pleasant to have such a large staff, but I must emphasize that all the jobs can be done, and frequently are, by far fewer people. Moreover, you might prefer to see a different chain of command, giving some of the Producer's responsibilities to the Stage Manager, for instance.

2

Choosing a Play

Who Chooses the Play?

Amateur groups differ considerably in the way they are con-
stituted and work, and this makes it impossible to lay down
any hard and fast rules about the selection of plays. Some
companies are run like a dictatorship, with a strong person-
ality at their head who is almost certainly the director of all
their productions. In that case the question does not arise; he
will choose the play and the rest of the group will accept the
choice, and that is an end to it. That system works very well,
provided that the dictator has the confidence of the other
members of the society and appreciates and gives weight to all
the factors that go into the choice of a play.

In other groups, mostly large companies with a number of
directors available, the choice may be made by the executive
committee. Having drawn up a programme of plays to be
performed during the next season, they will then set about
deciding who shall direct them, in the knowledge that among
the many potential directors there is almost bound to be at
least one person who will like and want to direct each play on
the list.

Most small amateur societies, with only one or two possible
directors, avoid either of these extremes, and their plays are
chosen, often with great difficulty, only after many people have
had their say. It is essential that the director, above all others,
should like the play, and indeed should be enthusiastic about
it. He is going to be the driving force behind the whole production, the person who has a vision of the final presentation
in mind which he is going to do his best to realize. It may
therefore make sense to decide first who is going to direct the
next production and let him take the preliminary steps towards

choosing the play to be performed. The preliminary steps only, because, if your director is an ordinary mortal rather than a dictator, he will want the support of the executive committee and indeed of the society as a whole if the show is to be a success. The committee may also feel a need, even if they do not express it publicly, to exercise some restraint on the director in question—perhaps he has a penchant for the kind of plays that neither your membership nor your audiences would enjoy. Once the director has a play in mind, it should be brought to the executive committee for their approval. It may even be worth putting it to the whole society, if this can be done conveniently—perhaps a series of playreadings could be arranged at which possible plays are tried out.

Another possibility is to appoint a play-selection sub-committee. One of their tasks might be to read and approve or disapprove plays submitted by a director, but their prime concern would probably be to look out for plays which would be suitable for the group.

Do make sure that the cast likes the play you are going to perform. Even professional actors will turn down parts in plays they dislike, but if, because their livelihood depends on it, they take part in such a play, they will probably try hard to make a go of it. On the whole amateurs don't do this, and if your cast is unenthusiastic you will find it very difficult to get the best out of them. If you have a very experienced company they may be able to give competent performances in a play that they dislike, but it is almost certain that the production will lack the sparkle that comes when the actors really enjoy the play.

In the end it does not matter a great deal which method of choosing a play you adopt, provided that the large majority of your members will support the choice.

Considerations in Choosing the Play

Availability and suitability of cast. It is a good idea to discover, if possible, who is available to take part in a play, and to help backstage, before even starting to decide what you will put on. There is no point in selecting *The Crucible*, with its cast of ten men and ten women, if you have only half a dozen actors. Equally, it would be difficult to produce *Zigger Zagger* if your membership, though large enough, is almost all middle-aged or elderly. And while it is true that there are comparatively few really good plays for all-women casts and one sympathizes with the dilemma of all-women groups, they should probably not risk the demands of male impersonation that a mixed cast would impose.

There are other problems too. You may have the right numbers and sexes to put on, for instance, *Private Lives*, but have you got actors with the ability to sustain the parts of Amanda and Elyot? Of course it may be that those available could, with good direction, make a tolerable shot at the characters, but you should at least be aware of the risks before settling on that play for your next production.

The staging of the play. Can you cope with the set or sets which the play demands? It may seem unambitious to stick to one-set plays, but that may be preferable to straining the resources of your stage staff too far (though it might be worth considering whether a multiple-set play could be staged suitably in a curtain set, using furniture and maybe a few pieces of scenery to suggest the various scenes without having to build a number of box sets). Is your stage large enough to accommodate the setting required and the number of actors involved? And what about costume? Costumes are expensive to hire, and though you may be able to make dresses for the women fairly simply, men's costumes are usually much more difficult to run up, however capable a team of sempstresses you may have.

The budget. How much will you have to spend on scenery, lighting, costumes, the hire of the hall, printing (publicity, tickets, programmes), royalties and any other necessary licences, plus other incidental expenses? If you can work out roughly what your box office takings are likely to be, you will be able to see whether you can afford to put the play on—or indeed whether to go ahead with a production which you expect to make a loss, because everyone in the group wants to do it and you have sufficient funds available not to bankrupt yourselves.

The suitability of the play for your audience. If you are, for instance, a church group, certain plays may be unsuitable for you because of the situations they show or the freedom of their language. It *is* possible to cut plays or alter words in them (deliberately, I mean—I am not referring to the changes resulting from imperfect learning of the lines), but it is essential to get the author's permission to do so. The publishers of the play can sometimes advise you whether or not permission is likely to be granted. Some authors raise no objections, while others will be very sticky indeed, as they have every right to be. And of course it will depend on exactly what you want to cut. It would have been little use to suggest to Shaw, for instance, that the famous 'bloody' in *Pygmalion* might be bowdlerized (the word is almost unexceptionable nowadays, and the scene has lost some of its strength as a result, but up to World War II and for some years after 'bloody' was still a shocking word, especially when used at an afternoon tea party in high society); if you had asked permission to cut it, it would have indicated that you did not understand Shaw's purpose in using it.

If you are one of those societies which, because of religious or other restrictions, find play selection a headache, it may be worth explaining your difficulty to the minister or other leader of the group with which you are associated—it is just possible that he will be willing to support you in being a little more venturesome. If, however, he insists on cuts or bans the whole play, your hackles may rise at such blatant censorship. If so, go and join a non-church society—there is no point in fighting.

If you decide to put on a play which will shock your audience, you will have a better chance of getting away with it if you prepare them for it by advance publicity, but you probably need to do something more than simply tell them that it is shocking, which may attract some, but which is likely to put more of them off. Explain why you are doing the play, what its merits are, perhaps what its message is. You may be able to reinforce what you say by quoting reviews of the play's professional production.

Should you, by the way, want to make cuts on the grounds that the play is too long, or that parts of it are boring, again you need permission to do so, unless the play is out of copyright (see page 24), in which case you may alter it as you please without fear of anything worse than the irate author's ghost returning to haunt you. Do be careful, however, not to mangle the play so badly as to destroy the playwright's intent.

'Our audience only likes comedies.' Yes, but that's no reason to give them nothing else. Equally, if you put on the kind of play from which the audience stays away in droves, then by all means carry on if you enjoy performing to rows of empty seats and can bear the costs involved. Though there is no sense in sticking to a rigid rota of different types of plays (comedy, drama, thriller, farce, comedy, drama, thriller, farce, comedy . . . etc.), a certain amount of variety is good for your players and for your audience. It *is* possible to educate an audience to enjoy and support different types of play, even if it requires much greater ticket-selling efforts to persuade them to come to something which they think is not their cup of tea.

The local competition.   Try to find out what other amateur societies in your area are doing or have done recently. Obviously it is not a good idea to put on the play which has just been produced by a nearby company, unless you can be sure that your audiences do not overlap at all. If they don't, it is just possible that there would be advantages, such as being able to borrow costumes or properties from the other group, but even then it is better to avoid duplication.

Choose a quality play.   Always choose the best play you can find which suits your other requirements. How do you recognize a good play? The fact that it has recently been a West End success does not guarantee its quality. A well-written play has good construction, strong characterization, believable and rhythmic dialogue, a plot or narrative which develops in an interesting way, and probably a message of some sort however well it may be concealed behind a façade of pure entertainment. Don't be misled by that word 'message'—I believe that the theatre's prime function is to entertain, not to preach. But entertainment depends in part on catharsis—the stimulation and purging of the audience's emotions by their vicarious experience of what is presented on the stage. Even the most frivolous of farces, if it is a good one, tells us something about the world we live in, about ourselves, about the human condition, and to that extent may be said to contain a message.

It may not be difficult to recognize a good plot and characters who are real and alive, engaging the audience's interest and sympathies, rather than mere puppets or caricatures, but the qualities of the construction and the rhythm of the dialogue may be harder to appreciate.

A well-constructed play can generally be broken down into a number of sections: the exposition, when the problem of the play and its characters are introduced, the complication, when the conflict emerges, the climax, the resolution and the conclusion. In many modern plays these divisions are not so clearly marked as in the past, but the basic framework is still there. A good play does not contain characters who do not contribute to the plot or theme; it does not use sub-plots which are unrelated to the main story; it does not cheat by the use of unfair coincidences or by the introduction of a *deus ex machina* (a term derived from the Greek theatre and used to mean a person who arrives at the end of a play to sort out all the problems that the characters face); it does not sag in the middle, but keeps the interest going throughout; it has well-spaced climaxes; it balances the elements which go to make up the action so that none of them is out of proportion to the rest; if it is a serious play it probably uses comedy to relieve tension, and then builds the drama to an even higher pitch; it breaks its scenes and acts at a moment of climax; it is consistent in its approach and to its own truth; and above all it presents conflict and contrast, without which there is no drama.

One other vital quality which might be mentioned is that a good play remains interesting to the director and the actors throughout the rehearsals, perhaps because of its sub-text— what it says beneath and beyond the surface of its action and dialogue—and because of the variety of interpretation and the challenge that it offers.

Plays are of course meant to be spoken, not simply read silently, so if you want to test the quality of the dialogue, read the play aloud. Listen for the characterization—in a good play for most of the time you will be able to tell who is speaking from the content of the lines alone. Listen for the rhythm of the writing—not a tum-ti-tum beat to the words, but a rightness of phrasing, a flow, a balance in the way the dialogue switches from one character to another. Good dialogue is easy to read at sight, because you will immediately realize where the emphasis should go, where to pause for breath, and what the thought behind the line is. Not the easiest thing to explain, these elements are readily recognizable if you have any kind of ear for the theatre.

However, if you find it difficult to assess the relative qualities of the plays you read, at least choose a well-known playwright. Whether he is one of the great names from the past or an acclaimed contemporary, he is unlikely to have gained his reputation without cause.

This does not mean you are confined in your choice to wordy, serious plays, to classics which your audience may find boring and which may also be very expensive to mount, or to possibly unintelligible experimental theatre. It simply means that if you want to put on a drawing-room comedy, you should choose the best drawing-room comedy you can find. The repertoire of good plays is enormous and varied.

The advantages of choosing a good play are that the actors will find the lines easier to learn (because of that rhythm) and will enjoy taking part, the shape of the play, its changes of mood and pace and its climaxes will be more readily perceptible to the director, and the audience will have better entertainment, and may even come in large numbers if they recognize the playwright's name.

You may feel that such a choice will be too ambitious, and the less experienced you are the less challenging your production should be. But the better the play, the more all concerned will learn from it, and the greater the chance you will have of getting away with sub-standard direction, acting and staging. It is like a carpet—the higher the quality, the more rough treatment it will stand. A really good play will somehow contrive to shine through an appalling production, and however inexperienced your actors may be, the better-written their parts are, the less likely it is that they will utterly ruin the play. Just think what extraordinary things even the professionals have done to Shakespeare without destroying his plays. Never be afraid to stretch yourself and your company.

Copyright

It should be emphasized that no performance of a play may be given in public, whether or not you charge for admission, or have admission by programme or by any device other than a ticket, or in the usual way by ticket, without the permission of the author or his agent (most play publishers act as agent for the plays they publish) and the payment of a fee, usually calculated per performance. Private performances are often subject to the same restrictions, the agent's definition of 'private' not necessarily being the same as yours. Plays are copyright and are the property of the author, who frequently depends for his living on the royalties he receives from performances of the work he has created. If the author has been dead for fifty years or more, copyright in the play has usually lapsed, but even then it is worth checking, because there are some exceptions, especially plays translated from foreign languages when the original play could be out of copyright but the translation very much in copyright. You are not even safe necessarily with plays in English by long-dead playwrights; the Royal Shakespeare Company, for instance, has adapted several seventeenth, eighteenth and nineteenth century plays, and their versions of them are in full copyright, at least until fifty years after the deaths of the adaptors. Check the copies of the play from which you are working, and if there is any mention of copyright or of the work having been adapted from the original, you will almost certainly have to get permission to perform it and pay a royalty. Fees are also payable for the performance of an extract from a copyright play and for public playreadings.

Before you make your final choice, it is also wise to find out from the publisher that the play in question is available for amateurs. The fact that the publisher has supplied copies does not necessarily guarantee this. It may be that the West End run of the play has not yet ended, or perhaps a London or touring company is putting on a revival of it. Professionals, reasonably enough, don't want competition from an amateur production of the same play, and amateur rights will therefore be restricted. Check first.

3

Casting the Play

Preparing for the Audition

Most amateur societies hold auditions. Attendance at an audition usually means a willingness to take part in the play, and in itself that is a good reason for holding one, though it is essential that the director should make clear at the very beginning when he intends to have rehearsals and when the performances will take place, in case any of the potential cast will not be available when required.

Before the audition it is necessary to acquire a number of copies of the play. If you have one or two copies only it makes for confusion. If you are certain of being able to put the play on, you should purchase in advance (checking that it is available for amateur performance on the dates of your production) sufficient copies for each member of the cast to have one, and extra copies for the director, the stage manager, the prompter and probably the stage, lighting and sound directors. If you should be entering the play in a festival, you will need an extra copy for the adjudicator. Please note that the photocopying of plays is illegal. You may be able, instead of buying copies, to borrow them; some amateur companies lend out sets, and many libraries do, and if you are not absolutely certain that the play in question will be produced it is obviously better to borrow than to buy for the purposes of the audition. The problem with borrowing copies is that you must not deface them, and since all the actors are likely to need to mark their copies, it has to be done very lightly in pencil and rubbed out before the books are returned.

Having obtained the copies, the director will need to choose the passages from the play which are to be read at the audition. In a large cast play he may not wish to waste time in auditioning the very small parts, but generally he will select passages so that every character can be heard. Where possible it is best to choose duologues, and certainly he should avoid passages with a whole string of characters each having only a few lines to say, though this may be inevitable in some cases. Two or three pages of script usually suffice to give some feel for the character, and the director should look for extracts which are typical of the characters concerned. For the main roles he will probably pick more than one passage, partly in order to avoid having to go over and over the same lines, but principally because the different extracts may show the characters in varying moods. If you choose highly dramatic moments, bear in mind that it is not always easy to gauge how an actor will play such a scene when he is reading it 'cold', for the first time, and without much idea of what the play is about.

Conducting the Audition

Some amateur companies send out newsletters, and if they do so in advance of the audition, can usefully include a description of the play and its characters, but even if this has been done, the director should start the audition by talking about the play and each of the parts in it—people don't always read newsletters! Then, taking one of his selected passages, he will either ask for volunteers to read or will ask certain members to do so, stopping them at the end of the extract and repeating the exercise with other candidates. After two or three such readings, he can pass on to a different set of characters and hear other actors. If need be, he can always return to an earlier passage to hear yet more potential players, but to read the same piece of the play several times in succession is not only boring but often leads those who are trying out for the parts to give extravagant readings in an effort to sound different from those who have read the same lines before them. When several people have read, he may want to return to some of the earlier candidates to hear their voices again, and at the end of the evening he should ask whether anyone present wants to read a part that they have not yet tried.

What Should the Director Look For?

The answer is obvious—a cast of actors who read the various parts as though they were made for them. It is rarely as easy as that, especially since many good amateur actors read badly if they have had no chance of preparing. Even if they read very well, the director must look upon them as raw material which he has to help turn into a finished product, so rather than expecting perfection, he will be listening for the right kind of voice for the character, a glimmer of understanding of the role, and a sense that, at least for the major roles, the actors suggest that they have the authority to carry the part.

He will also have some regard to age and physical appearance. Of course, actors can and often do play outside their own ages—some play older characters from the beginning to the end of their acting careers, while others get away with juvenile parts when they are well past middle-age—and miracles of ageing or rejuvenation can be achieved with make-up (though this is not always effective in the amateur theatre since the strength of lighting is not usually brilliant enough to disguise it). An additional problem can arise with an audience many of whom will be aware of the actor's true age. I remember acting an older man at the age of eighteen or so; I had been quite skilfully made up and coached carefully to look and sound as mature as possible, but when I announced in the play, 'I'm forty-seven,' the audience fell about.

Physical characteristics, except perhaps in matters of age, should not matter too much, provided that the actors concerned have some talent. I can think of two marvellous performances given by inappropriately shaped actors in plays that I directed. One was a tall but very much overweight player taking the lead of John Proctor in *The Crucible*—indeed, I hope he won't mind if I call him fat. Now, fat people on stage are usually buffoons, or possibly villainous, but Peter was a good enough actor for one to forget his shape, and I believe that if you had asked the members of the audience after the play, they would have said that he was a big man, but would not have said he was fat. The other example was the part of Cornelius in *The Matchmaker*, who is both comic and romantic and who was played by an actor who is very short,

with a Mrs Molloy and a Barnaby who towered over him.
Again, Keith played the role with such style and humour and
inner conviction that his lack of inches became totally unimportant.

Equally, if you are casting a play which is particularly associated with a famous actor with well-known characteristics—
Robert Morley, for instance—you don't have to find someone
who looks like him, nor should you allow the actor who plays
the part to try to reproduce Mr Morley's delivery and style of
acting, which he will almost certainly fail to do convincingly. I
cite Mr Morley for good reason, having once played one of his
most successful roles—Frank Foster in Alan Ayckbourn's
How the Other Half Loves. I found it very difficult indeed. I
could hear Robert Morley's voice in virtually every line, and
floundered unhappily through the rehearsals trying not to ape
him. Only in the last couple of weeks did I find my own
characterization of the part. No doubt a professional actor
would have had less trouble than I did, but I managed it in the
end, and many people thought it the best thing I had ever done.
Sorry for the immodesty, but the point behind it is, I think,
worth making.

Something to look out for at the audition is eagerness to play
a certain part. It may be that the actor showing this is quite
unsuitable in your view, but if you have to choose between two
apparently equal candidates, take the eager one.

You may know many of your potential cast well, and be
fully aware of their capabilities. If so, at least try them in parts
which are different from those they normally play for your
group. The challenge will probably interest them, and casting
against the stereotype can sometimes work very well.

If you don't know any of the potential cast or have new-
comers at the audition, you will have to listen and assess with
extra care, remembering not only that some actors read less
well than they act, but that others read well at the audition and
never develop at all.

Absentees

Almost inevitably some candidates for the cast will not have
been able to come to the audition. When you announce the

date of the audition, you should make provision for this eventuality, asking such people to indicate in advance if they are nevertheless interested in having a part. You may need to hold an additional audition if there are many such absentees, or a private one for perhaps one or two, even if you know their capabilities, because it is important to be seen to be treating everyone alike.

But supposing you don't get enough people at your audition to cast the play and none of those who are missing has informed you that they would like to take part? Well, you can either abandon that play and find one with a smaller cast, or try getting in touch with all the absentees and twisting their arms, or you can perhaps borrow members from other societies, if both they and the societies are willing. I remember that the late L. du Garde Peach once described in *Amateur Stage* how he had put on a play with a very large cast despite the fact that his group did not have enough members to fill all the parts, simply by approaching friends and neighbours and cajoling or browbeating them into acting for him. I rather suspect that it was difficult to refuse L. du Garde Peach anything, and if you have the same sort of charisma you may be able to follow his example. Otherwise, it's back to the drawing-board.

When to Announce the Cast

It saves a lot of trouble if you can announce the cast at the end of the audition. The first rehearsal can be fixed, the actors can take their copies of the play (not that many of them will do anything other than look at their own parts before the read-through), and you may have the chance of appointing some of the backstage staff from among those who will not be acting. If because of absentees or for some other reason you cannot finalize the cast, though you may be able to give out some of the parts, you should announce firmly when the casting will be completed. 'If you have not heard from me by the end of the week, you can take it that, much as I would like to have you in the play, I haven't been able to include you this time. I shall probably be asking some of you to help backstage, and I hope you will agree to do so.' If you are not announcing any of the cast at the audition, remember to collect in all the copies of the play.

Always make your final announcement of the cast at the earliest possible date, for everybody's sake, including your own.

Should the Director have the Sole Responsibility for Casting?

It depends first of all on whether he knows at least the majority of those attending the audition. If he is a guest director, he will probably need the advice of senior members of the society. However, even if he does not have that problem, I am very much in favour of using a Casting Committee, which should consist of the director and two others, of which one should be the stage manager if he has already been appointed. The director is all powerful on this committee, and although he should listen carefully to the opinions of the other two, which can often be very useful, can overrule them if he wants to. Then why have a committee? Principally because it gives disgruntled members of the society less opportunity to blame a single person (the director) for the fact that they have not been given the parts they wanted.

When Not to Have an Audition

Some groups feel that auditions are no more than a cosmetic device to make it appear that the group is a democracy and that everyone has a chance of playing any kind of part, whereas in practice it is either a dictatorship under the control of the director, or the casting is predetermined simply because the group tends to put the same people in the same kind of parts in every production (which suggests a fairly small company, rather like the old touring players with their stock descriptions of their members—'heroine', 'low comedian', 'character old woman', 'heavy father', etc). Nevertheless, I feel that auditions are worth holding, especially because very few that I have been concerned with have turned out to be as much of a foregone conclusion as might have been expected. New members show their paces; others whom you had thought you would cast are not after all available; your 'heavy father' suddenly seems a much better prospect as the 'low comedian'.

But there have been cases when I have directed a play and announced in advance that there would be no audition for a certain character. For instance, when my group put on *Charley's Aunt* it was quite obvious that we had one candidate only, and a very good one too, for the leading role of Lord Fancourt Babberley. If he had not been available to play the part, I could not have envisaged anyone else in the society doing so, and would have abandoned the play. So before the audition I made sure that he was available and willing, and then announced that I had already cast that one part.

Some societies find that it works quite well for them to hold auditions for their full-length productions, but to cast one-act plays by invitation from the director concerned.

A Final Thought

However tempted you may be to emulate the great actor managers, it is usually a major mistake to cast yourself in a play which you are directing, even in a tiny part. You have enough to worry about without having to learn lines and perfect your performance, but quite apart from that, it is almost impossible for you to see the production as a whole, to be sure that when you yourself are on stage the grouping is right, to ensure that the play is properly balanced.

Of course it is often done, and successfully too, and it may be the only way that you will manage to put the play on. If you are forced into the position of being simultaneously director and actor, the stage manager really must act as assistant director and keep a special watch on those scenes in which you appear.

4

The Director's Preparation

Organization

The director is in charge of the entire production. Within any limits laid down by the society or its committee, he will have a completely free hand with every aspect of the play, so he will not only conduct rehearsals, in which he will impose his concept of the style of the production, but will also have approval of everything from set design to programme. It is because he has so much responsibility that I have already suggested the appointment of two principal assistants, the stage manager and the producer. The director will delegate more or less of his responsibility to these two assistants according to personal taste. In practice, most amateur shows demand a great deal from the director, and the more chores he can pass to others, the better for his health and sanity.

Of course, the stage manager and the producer need to be people with whom he can work amicably. An essential part of delegation is having trust in your subordinates and leaving them to get on with their jobs, with direction, but without interference. Select your staff with care, and your task will be much easier.

The Production Meeting

Having chosen a play, and if necessary obtained the executive committee's approval to go ahead with it, the director should call a production meeting of all those in charge of the various aspects of the presentation, as listed in Chapter One. This meeting will probably take place after the audition, by which time the director may hope to know which members are undertaking the different backstage jobs.

If possible, everyone attending the meeting should have read the play beforehand, so that the discussion can be effective. I do mean *discussion*. The director must always be prepared to alter his ideas about anything to do with the production, both now and later, in the light of good suggestions from other people or practical problems which arise.

The meeting should end with everyone knowing exactly what they are expected to do and when, and a schedule of events should be drawn up, showing the dates by which all such matters as set design, set building, hire of costumes, opening of box office, and so on, should be completed or done.

The Producer

The director must ensure that the producer leaves the production meeting fully briefed on all the aspects of the production which will come under his control. If this is done, there will probably be no need of any further formal meetings of the production committee.

If you follow the list of officials and the chain of command suggested in Chapter One, it will be the producer's responsibility to appoint a number of heads of department and to oversee their work. Whether separate persons are required for each of these jobs depends on the complexity of the play and the number of helpers available. In many cases, the producer himself may take on certain of the functions. He will liaise constantly with those who report to him, and keep the director informed of progress, of any developments which are a departure from the original plan, and will see that everything is proceeding to time and that there are no unsolved problems.

He will also be responsible for obtaining a licence to perform the play (which should be done at an early stage), a licence from the local authority for public performances, and any other necessary permissions and authorizations for such matters as the use of music or of firearms.

The Style of Production

Before he can begin rehearsals, or indeed hold the production meeting, the director needs to know the play thoroughly, and

will have read it many times. When he has done so, he will
know the story of the play, he will know the characters, he will
probably be able to visualize much of the action. But he must
know far more than that. Above all, he has to recognize the
author's intention, the mood of the play and the style it
demands. This is essential if he is to carry out effectively the
director's job, one definition of which is to interpret the play to
the audience.

Deciding on the author's intention and settling on the mood
and style of the play may seem very easy and elementary, but
there are pitfalls. For instance, *The Lion in Winter* is a serious
play, full of dramatic conflict, but it is overlaid with a marvellous wit and sense of fun which, far from detracting from the
drama, enhances it. But in an amateur production which I saw
not long ago the director had not seen the humour in the play,
or if he had been aware of it had not been able to persuade his
cast to project it. Always ask yourself not only why the playwright wrote the play, but why he wrote it the way he did and
how he meant it to be played.

There are many other problems of style, and they demand a
considerable knowledge of the theatre from the director. If you
are going to put on an old-fashioned melodrama, you need to
know the conventions with which it should be performed—the
exaggerated movements, the asides to the audience, the heavily
pointed dialogue. Well, most of us have some idea about that,
but we may be less confident in, say, Restoration comedy,
which requires an equally formal and mannered presentation,
and the director must be familiar with the correct approach if
he is to make a success of the production. It is not only in
period plays that different styles are needed—you would not
present an Ayckbourn play in the same manner as one by
Pinter, for instance.

The mood and style of the play will almost certainly affect
the director's view of the characters. Their realization is going
to be a joint effort between him and the actors, but he is the one
who has to shape them and weld them together, and it is
essential for him to see them clearly and to understand their
relationships with each other. The actor often tends to be
selfish in that he is only concerned with the character he is
playing; the director has to see that all the characters are

played so that the author's intention is realized and interpreted effectively, without any one character throwing the play out of balance. It will certainly help him, and he will be able to use the material at the audition and later for the guidance of the actors, to make a summary of the characteristics of each person in the play, perhaps picking out particularly significant lines in the text which are revealing of the character who is speaking or the one he is speaking about.

Analysing the Play

Even if you think you know the play well, read it again—at least a couple of times. Study the means by which the playwright puts his story and his points across. Break the play down into its components—exposition, complication, climax, resolution and conclusion—and see how each section is constructed. Split the components further into units involving a theme or mood or a certain group of characters. Incidentally, this will also be of use at rehearsals, allowing you to see the sections to concentrate on, and the actors to understand the structure and rhythm of the play and their roles in it more clearly. In each case ask yourself what the author's intention was—what are the important points that have to be established, whose scene it is, how you are going to ensure that the audience sees that section in the way you want them to.

It is always interesting, by the way, to work out whose scene it is. Usually one character dominates, but every so often dominance passes to someone else, even in a duologue. If you read the play carefully, you will be able to say, 'These three pages are A's scene. These ten lines are B's.'

Look too for places where the play changes direction, as it were, and for major and minor climaxes. Plays move from one crisis or moment of intensity to another, and the tension must rise and fall continuously, but each peak, though followed by a trough, is moving us towards another peak, and eventually on to the main climax of the play. There must be a sense of driving towards that main peak, with the tension building and the troughs never becoming so deep that the audience loses interest. Note that after an interval the audience's attention and interest has to be recaptured, so it is essential to begin the new scene or act by re-establishing the sense of urgency and purpose.

The changes of direction (which occur perhaps when a new character comes on stage, or a new theme or mood is introduced into the dialogue) and the climaxes are tremendously important. Handle them well, and the play will get across to the audience effectively. The director must therefore work on such moments most carefully, planning exactly how to achieve the results he needs. Very often it is a matter of pace (the speed with which the actors pick up their cues) which may need to be fast or slow, perhaps with one or two quite long pauses. The tone of the actors' voices and their facial expressions and their reactions will also contribute, and their positions on the stage can be most important in moments of tension. A good director usually knows instinctively how to get the effect he wants, but he should also work out why he wants a certain pace or tone or mood because it will be easier to direct such moments if he can explain rationally to the cast not only how the scene must be played, but why.

The work that you do at this stage on the crucial moments of the play should bring the additional reward of allowing you to see more clearly how, in contrast, the rest of the play should be directed. Look for variety of tone, pace, colour, grouping within the moments of tension, and in the play as a whole. Make your actors aware of the need for variety too, especially in long speeches. But be sure always that the changes derive from the structure of the play and the dialogue and the thoughts behind it. Constant variety for its own sake can result in a busy, confusing effect—let it come where the play demands it.

The Staging

Most amateurs work from acting editions which usually contain a plan of the scenes, showing the position of entrances and furniture. Very often amateur companies have little hope of producing anything remotely resembling the professional set, when their stage is a quarter the size of that in a professional theatre, has no wings and the only possible entrance is from one upstage corner. You have to adapt, and you should never be afraid to do so. Read the play and decide what setting and furniture is indispensable and possible with the facilities available to you.

Of course, before planning the set the director must be familiar with the stage on which it is to be performed—the amount of space, the size of the wings, whether it is possible to get from one side of the stage to the other without being seen by the audience, and other details of this kind. Don't despair if the stage seems quite inadequate. I know an amateur society which puts on Gilbert and Sullivan with a cast of thirty or more on a very small stage to which there are only two entrances— up left and down left—and no wings at all. If the backcloth were brought forward to allow for a passage behind it, there would not be enough room on stage to accommodate the chorus. Yet meticulous staging allows their problems to be unnoticeable to the majority of the audience, and only those in the know are aware that if a character goes off stage right he is going to have to stay there in a space which barely gives him room to breathe until his next entrance or the interval.

Very few plays are incapable of being set by a company with a postage stamp of a stage. Even if you can't reproduce a baronial hall, you may be able to suggest one corner of it, or even if you would find it impossible to attempt the four luxurious interiors demanded by *The First Gentleman*, you may be able to play the whole thing in curtains, using a few ornaments, statues, chandeliers and the like to suggest both the atmosphere and the change of scene.

At this early stage it is also important to try to work out your lighting. You may not understand much of the technicalities, but you can at least decide on the kind of effect you want and ask the lighting director if he can provide it. The lighting may influence your decisions on the positions and movements of the actors, and vice versa.

Preparing Your Copy of the Play

You will now be thinking about marking your copy of the play in various ways. You will probably want to indicate changes of direction and the climaxes and other moments of particular intensity, important lines, pauses, places where the pace has to be fast and others where it can be taken more slowly, passages which you think will be particularly difficult for the actors, moments when the reactions of those on stage will be important, cues for lighting changes and sound effects. There is no end to the number of reminders of this sort that you can mark in the script, though some directors, unwisely I think, prefer to carry it all in their heads, or to improvise it as the rehearsals proceed. There is certainly something to be said for leaving room for your instinct to work, and you will doubtless wish to add to your notes or alter them as the production develops, but detailed preparation is invaluable.

Of course, if you make a great many marks on the printed pages of the play, even if you use different coloured inks to mean different things, your script will soon be almost illegible—and we have not even begun to consider positions, grouping, moves and business. The solution is to interleave the pages of your copy with blank sheets of paper on which to make notes.

Positions

At this point it would be as well to clarify the terms used to describe positions on the stage. The following diagram shows them:

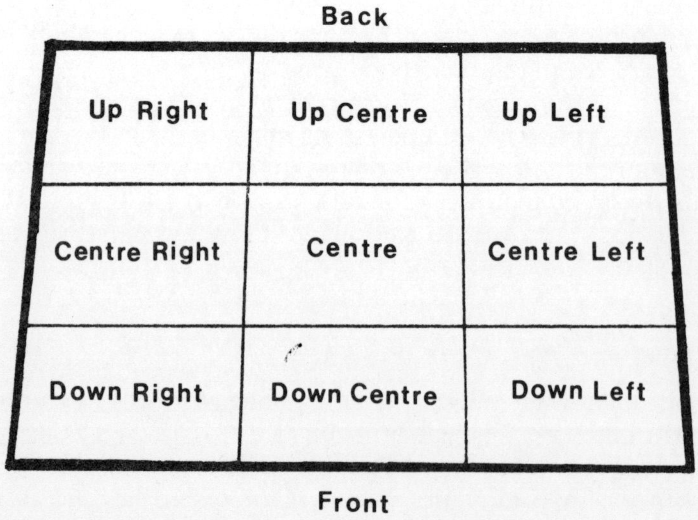

Back

Up Right	Up Centre	Up Left
Centre Right	Centre	Centre Left
Down Right	Down Centre	Down Left

Front

Note that right and left are always given from the actor's point of view as he faces the audience. Upstage is 'up' because when the terms were first used most professional stages were fairly steeply raked, and therefore the back of the stage was 'up' and the front was 'down'.

Various positions on the stage are stronger, more dominant than others. The centre third of the stage is stronger than either left or right, and for reasons of which no one is quite sure, right is stronger than left. Downstage is usually stronger than upstage, though if you have three or more actors on stage arranged, however roughly, in a triangle, the actor at its upstage apex will normally have the dominant position. Even so, except for an entrance, the strength begins to fade once you are more than about two-thirds of the way back. So the order of importance is really downstage centre, centre, upstage centre, downstage right, downstage left, centre right, centre left, upstage right, upstage left.

According to this theory, if you have two actors on the stage and place one upstage and the other downstage, the latter should be dominant. He will be, unless he has to turn to the upstage actor for most or all of the dialogue. The downstage actor is being 'upstaged' by the other, and that is a weak position. If you want the upstage actor to be the dominant one, such positioning is fine, but you must not leave the other poor fellow with his back to the audience for too long. He may have a rear view which, like Katisha's right elbow, has a fascination which few can resist, but the spectators will soon get bored with it, and will also probably find it difficult to hear what he says. So, particularly if it is a long duologue, place the two actors on the same level.

Now, the actor's full face is very much stronger than his profile (which in turn, obviously, is stronger than the head turned away from the audience), but it will look very unnatural to have them both facing fully front all the time, and rather dull if they are continuously in profile. Turn them a quarter towards the audience. Of course, the actors can still look straight out front from time to time, or away from the person to whom they are talking. Although a certain amount of eye contact between the actors is desirable, we do not look at people we are talking to during every second of a conversation.

When you are working out positions and moves, think of the stage as divided into acting areas, and try to use them all, being aware of their relative strengths and weaknesses and concentrating the important action in the most dominant sections.

Remember too the advantage of isolating your characters if they are separated by their thoughts or actions. For instance, if you are staging the trial scene from *Saint Joan*, it is more effective to place Joan on her own down right than to give her the apparently more dominant position centre stage, when her accusers and judges will be seen as surrounding her and you will lose the effect of conflict and the imbalance between their massed ranks and her own solitary figure. The eyes of the audience are very sensitive to positions and groupings and will pick up the unspoken significance of the various pictures that you present to them.

Something else which gives emphasis is height, and if you are using rostra, which also have the great advantage of adding variety to your set and to the moves, this is another point to bear in mind.

You must also take into account the sight-lines. In many halls, the audience sitting on the sides of the front rows may not be able to see the full stage, and you must therefore avoid placing any highly significant parts of the action where the sight-lines would make it invisible to them, quite apart from the fact that such areas will usually be dramatically weak in any case. If your hall has a balcony, remember that the back of the stage may be cut off from the sight of the audience seated there by the proscenium arch and any valences you are using.

Grouping

All that has been said about positions affects the way you arrange the grouping when you have several actors on the stage at the same time. Those whose scene it is or who have a key line to speak or an important piece of action to perform must be in a strong position.

Apart from such considerations you must always try to place your actors so that the grouping is pleasant to look at, and varied. Avoid masking as far as possible—that is to say, placing actors in positions where they are concealed from the audience by other actors or by furniture. Also avoid letting the characters stand in straight lines, which not only look strangely unnatural but attract the eyes of the audience and lead them to look in the direction that the line is pointing.

One of the most difficult problems a director faces in arranging his actors is the scene at a dining table. To place them all on the upstage side of the table may make them visible to the audience, but looks extremely unnatural, while if some have their backs to the audience, their faces cannot be seen, they may become less audible and they may mask the actors on the other side of the table. If you must seat the actors on either side, at least put the table at an angle rather than sideways on to the front of the stage, or try setting it end on, and seating the actors on the short upstage end and the two sides. If you cannot even do this, you may be able to devise some way of letting one or more of the actors get up and move away from the table now and then. This is one case where it is certainly worth looking at the acting edition's stage directions and plan, for the professional director of the play may have solved the problem satisfactorily.

Moves

Since certain positions on the stage are stronger than others, it follows that moves are in themselves strong or weak according to the change in the position of the actor that results. So, a move from up right to down left is stronger than one in the opposite direction, but from up left to down right is stronger than from up right to down left. However, just to make things more complicated, a diagonal move is usually more effective than one across the stage from one side to the other, or from front to back (though the latter can suggest urgency). It all sounds desperately confusing, but if you work it out on the stage, you will see what I mean.

The most important thing to remember is that no move should be made without a reason. The majority of moves will probably suggest themselves quite adequately in the text—'he gets a drink from the table', 'he goes to her and kisses her', 'she goes to the window and looks out', etc. But some moves, even if they are indicated in the acting edition, do not have any

obvious motive, but have perhaps been introduced to break up
an otherwise static section of the play. Well, static sections do
need breaking up if they go on too long, but you should
examine the suggested moves carefully and see if they can be
justified in some way. In a long duologue where no move is
needed except to give the audience a change of picture to look
at, it may be possible to find a point in the lines where there is
sufficient tension to justify one of the characters moving, and
indeed an invented move of this kind may heighten the drama.

Never feel that you have to copy slavishly the moves indicated in the acting edition. Use them if they are good, discard
or change them if they are not or if they do not suit your
production.

As a general rule, it is better to cross the stage in front of
furniture than behind it, though of course there are occasions
when the actor must take the shortest route to wherever he has
to go. As for crossing in front of or behind other actors, this
will depend on whose scene it is and, again as a general rule, the
more dominant actor in that scene may cross in front of those
who are less important, but they should not cross in front of
him.

Always avoid moving characters from opposite sides of the
stage so that they cross one another. This is known as a scissors
movement. The reason it is wrong is that it confuses the
audience, who do not know which of the two actors to watch.

You will almost certainly need to consider whether or not
you will allow characters to move while they are speaking.
This will probably depend on the importance of what they are
saying. A line spoken while the actor is crossing the stage
usually has far less impact than if he is standing still. In real life
we tend to eschew movement when we have something
important to say. Try the effect of moving before the line is
said, during it, and after speaking. The first of these is much the
strongest, the second tends to diminish the importance of what
is said, while the third puts rather more emphasis on the move
than on the speech. And what about one character moving
while another is speaking? Be very wary of this, because the
move will almost certainly take the audience's attention away
from what is being said.

One other point to bear in mind is that you may have to

make certain allowances for the physical problems of your cast. If, for instance, you have a very elderly person in the play, it is unreasonable to expect him to stand for long periods at a time if you can contrive a legitimate reason to move him to a seat for part of the scene. And of course the elderly often find it difficult to move quickly.

Entrances and Exits

The first entrance of characters in the play, or any dramatic re-appearance, must be planned with care, especially for the principal roles, so that those in the audience have a clear view and their attention is focused on the entrance. The most powerful entrance will be centre back, but wherever it is, the grouping of the other players on stage must be such that the entrance is not masked. The same applies to important exits.

It can sometimes be effective to bring characters on or let them exit through the auditorium, but it is a device which needs to be used sparingly, principally because it weakens the convention that what takes place on stage behind the proscenium arch is in fact reality. By allowing the actors to appear among the audience you are presenting a different form of reality, and though the intention is to give the spectators a greater sense of participation, I feel that only rarely does it achieve this, and usually only in plays such as *On Monday Next* where the whole theatre is, to some extent, considered as a stage.

Business

Business is the word used to describe actions, usually of a fairly elaborate nature, frequently involving properties and un-accompanied by explanatory dialogue. The stage direction 'she hands him a letter' can hardly be described as business, but if he then looks at it in surprise, hastily puts it in his pocket, takes it out again, begins to open it, changes his mind, drops it, picks it up and stares at it again, and finally hands it back to her, saying, 'You open it for me,' that might be described as 'business with letter'. Very often the stage directions will say no more than 'business with letter', and you will have to work out what is actually done.

Business can be serious or funny, and may be of vital importance in the play. It is nearly always a major ingredient of farces.

You may feel that you cannot work out business properly until you have the actors and the properties with which to do it, and it may be true that an element of improvisation during rehearsals will suggest how it should be done, but at least at this stage you should begin to have ideas about it. Actors will sometimes bring imaginative touches to business, as to the rest of their parts, but in the early days they are inevitably rather script-bound, and if you can sketch out the business at the early rehearsals it will probably help their imaginations, and yours, to work on it later.

Focusing the Audience's Attention

In considering positions, grouping, moves, what we are really concerned with is the way you focus the audience's attention. You need to think about this all the time, and arrange your actors and the action to get the desired effect. Remember these vital points: movement on stage always attracts attention (so you will want to ensure that the audience is never distracted by unimportant movement); the audience looks where the actors look (so you can sometimes turn a less dominant position into a strong one if all the other actors on stage are looking in that direction); the audience wants to be able to see the characters clearly, especially the face of the actor whose scene it is, and they must have an unimpeded view of any vital movements, business or properties that are important to the action; an audience finds it difficult to take in more than one thing at a time, and if several things have to go on simultaneously, try to ensure that their attention is focused, by means of grouping and the other actors' reactions, on the most important.

Plotting the Moves

One of the best ways of working out moves is to draw yourself a fairly large plan of the stage, showing all the entrances and furniture. Take a Halma man, or something similar, for each person in the cast, marking them to distinguish one from the other. Read through the play, moving the Halma men on your plan whenever the characters in the play move. If you now draw small diagrams of the stage at various points in the play, you can show the positions of the actors, and their moves by means of arrows. Provided you either make a note beside the diagrams, or have the moves fixed firmly in your mind, you can record several changes of position in one drawing. For instance:

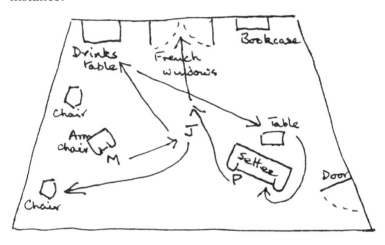

Malcolm gets up from easy chair, goes up to John. On 'I need a drink' goes to drinks table. After 'Sure you won't have one?' John goes to chair down right, sits. Malcolm to table behind settee, lights cigarette. Penny goes up centre, says line, exits French windows. At bottom of page Malcolm sits left side of settee.

In practice, your sketch will probably be much smaller and even rougher than the one above, you will not need to label the furniture, and your notes can be considerably briefer.

If you go through the play with care, working out positions and moves and groupings, you will find it easy at the first blocking rehearsal (that is, the rehearsal when you tell the actors their positions and moves) to give the instructions with the authority and confidence of a good director.

It is often difficult to work it all out with perfect accuracy, especially since you cannot always be sure of the exact size of

the furniture and your diagrams may not bear much relationship to the true proportions. Or you may find that you have
forgotten some vital move, or left an actor in an awkward
position, or that the reality makes a much uglier picture than
you had thought. Or again it may be that once you discuss the
play with other people and especially when in rehearsal the
actors begin to make their individual contributions, you will
change your mind about this or that or many things. You
should always be ready to be flexible, but my own view is that
if any doubts are in your mind, rather than felt by the cast, you
should not try to put the problem right there and then, which
might involve quite a waste of time while you agonize over the
solution, and will make you appear undecided in your role of
director. It is better, I think, simply to carry on with your
original movement and grouping plan, see what happens in the
next page or two of the play, and have another go at it before
the next rehearsal, so that you can announce any revised moves
confidently the next time you rehearse the scene.

5

Rehearsals

THE DIRECTOR

How Many Rehearsals and When

The timing of the rehearsals depends chiefly on the availability of the cast. Some societies have regular rehearsal days (for example, every Tuesday and Thursday), and that is excellent, because the actors know where they are, and the booking of rehearsal space is simplified; on the other hand, I always prefer to increase the number of rehearsals per week as the performance approaches, which means going outside regular dates. The most important thing is to make it clear as soon as possible, preferably at the audition, when you intend to rehearse, so that you get a commitment from your cast to attend.

The number of rehearsals you need depends on the experience of the players, the size of the cast, and especially the complexity of the play. Although amateur productions often appear to be under-rehearsed, in fact this often has less to do with having too few rehearsals than with the reluctance of many amateur actors to work between rehearsals, not only in learning their lines, but in studying the play as a whole, working on their characterizations, and practising their gestures and movements. I have known a full-length play put on by amateurs with as many as forty-two rehearsals; the production was well polished, but so many sessions did make tremendous demands on the keenness of the cast, and directors have to remember that not all may be quite as enthusiastic as they themselves or willing to give up so much time.

The ideal number of rehearsals will give the cast (and stage staff) total confidence in themselves and in each other—they

will know their lines, moves and business and what contri-
bution they have to make to the play as a whole—but they will
not have become stale. Plays in performance need a quality of
freshness about them, as though each time they are being acted
for the first time, but amateurs sometimes find it difficult to
maintain their sparkle if there have been too many rehearsals,
even with an audience to stimulate them. If your cast shows
signs of boredom—often manifest at the later rehearsals in a
lack of concentration, late entrances, the forgetting of lines
which they have previously known perfectly, and so on—it
may be wise to cancel the next rehearsal in order to give them a
break. But of course the director needs to feel confident that
the play has reached a stage when the cancellation will not do
more harm than good.

On the whole, I feel that most full-length plays need a
minimum of twenty rehearsals, plus two dress rehearsals and a
staging, lighting and sound rehearsal if there are many changes
and effects.

If you are directing a three-act play and rehearse an act at a
time in regular rotation, you will probably find that in the early
days when you rehearse an act again, your cast will have
forgotten most of what you told them the last time. Moreover,
the actors tend to learn their lines from the beginning of the
play onwards, so that working on the earlier scenes is often
more productive during the first rehearsals. For these reasons,
though there are no hard and fast rules, I like to work on a
programme of this kind:

1st rehearsal:	Read-through with all cast
2nd:	Act 1 blocking
3rd:	Act 2 blocking
4th:	Act 1
5th:	Act 2
6th:	Act 1
7th:	Act 3 blocking
8th:	Act 2
9th:	Act 3
10th:	Act 1, no scripts
11th:	Act 3
12th:	Act 2, no scripts
13th:	Act 3, no scripts

14th:	Act 1
15th:	Act 2
16th:	Act 3
17th:	Acts 1 and 2
18th:	Acts 3 and 1
19th:	Acts 2 and 3
20th:	Acts 1, 2 and 3
21st:	Acts 1, 2 and 3
22nd:	Staging rehearsal
23rd:	Dress rehearsal
24th:	Dress rehearsal

You will see from this plan that in the early stages I concentrate on Acts 1 and 2. When Act 3 is introduced the gaps between rehearsals of Acts 1 and 2 lengthen, and there is a danger here that the cast will slip back from the level they have reached previously, but generally the schedule seems to work well.

Of course, your play may not be divided into three acts, or you may find it convenient to make divisions in the play which do not relate to the acts or scenes, but are perhaps based on the characters. So you might say that a rehearsal would be for all the short bits, dotted throughout the play, for characters A, B and C. It sounds a messy way of working, but early rehearsals are pretty disorganized anyway, and you may find it pays dividends to concentrate on one or two of your principals, or a number of the smaller parts for an entire evening.

You should arrange rehearsals so that each time you call the minimum number of actors required. Most amateurs are glad of a night off, and nothing disgruntles them more than to come to a rehearsal and spend the whole evening waiting in vain to get to their bit. It often helps to announce that the rehearsal will start, say, with everyone who appears in the first section of the act, while those who come on in the second part need not arrive until an hour later.

If you have the opportunity of adding extra rehearsals, you may find it useful in the later stages to have one or two for 'diabolical bits'—that is, those parts of the play which most need attention—or for word rehearsals, at which the players simply concentrate on getting their lines right, without movement or, sometimes, any attempt at characterization or variety.

When to Insist that Books should no longer be Used

The majority of amateur actors are very slow at learning their lines, and indeed there are many who cannot be persuaded to make a serious attempt to do so until the final rehearsals arrive. The director's job is made much more difficult when half his cast is still carrying books, and he must insist firmly that on a given date, which should be indicated on the rehearsal schedule, they should know their words. Read the riot act in advance to any in the cast who have not made much progress. In a three-act play, one might say, as has been suggested in the rehearsal schedule above, that no books would be used for any act on the fourth occasion that it is rehearsed.

How Long Should Rehearsals Go On?

For most amateur groups, though this may not apply to all-women societies, it is often very difficult to start rehearsals before eight o'clock in the evening, and since most of those taking part will already have spent a busy day, two or perhaps two and a half hours is likely to be the maximum effective time that you can spend, after which the cast tends to get tired and anxious to get home, and loses concentration. It is not very long, but a prompt start and a determination on everybody's part to work hard can compensate for the comparatively early finish. In the later stages of rehearsal it will almost certainly be necessary to have longer rehearsals, and the cast should be warned of this in advance.

Starting Rehearsals On Time

It is extremely difficult to get amateurs to start rehearsals on time. Call a rehearsal for eight o'clock, and you will be lucky if you can start at a quarter past. I have found it works fairly well to make a bargain with a cast that I am directing: 'If we start on time at eight o'clock,' I say, 'we shall finish promptly at ten (or I might make it ten-fifteen or ten-thirty); if we are late starting, we shall finish when I am ready, which will probably be at least half an hour later.' If this is agreed to, I stick to it rigidly, ending the rehearsal sharp on the stated time, even if it is in the middle of a scene, or at least not continuing without asking the actors' permission. When possible I stop the rehearsal five minutes before the deadline, so that there is time for me to make any comments on what we have been doing.

There is no point in getting your actors to rehearsals promptly if you then dilly-dally. The beginning of a rehearsal is not the time for discussion of the set, the costumes, or anyone's personal problems. Get the cast down to work at once, and leave the chat either to the coffee break or to the end of the rehearsal.

Where to Rehearse

Where you rehearse again depends on circumstances. The ideal is to use the stage on which you will be performing, but comparatively few amateur groups are able to indulge in such luxury, and indeed many do not get on to the stage until the dress rehearsal. The next best thing is to rehearse in a space which is large enough—a small hall, perhaps—for you to mark out the full area of the stage on the floor with chalk, or to define it by rows of chairs to mark its edges, with gaps for the entrances. The next alternative is a room which may not offer a suitable area but which can at least be cleared of furniture. This may be a class-room, or a meeting-room, or even a room in a private house. Finally, there is the possibility of using a society member's sitting-room, full of furniture which cannot be moved out of it.

It is very difficult to rehearse the trial scene from *The Crucible*, for instance, with fourteen people on stage simultaneously, in a 14 × 11 ft room containing a three-piece suite, a couple of bookcases, a coffee table, a television set and a piano—but it can be done. It has been done. Obviously it is very far from ideal, but quite a lot can still be achieved. You might think that under such circumstances it would be better simply to sit down and have a word rehearsal, but movement of a kind is possible and is helpful, and I don't see that it is really much more difficult for an actor to imagine himself crossing the full width of the stage than to imagine himself to be a farmer from Salem, Massachusetts, in the year 1692.

One of the dangers when rehearsing in a hall or meeting-room is that you will use the available chairs to represent the furniture in your play. Three hall chairs in a line can do duty as a settee, and in width they may not be too far off the mark, but in depth they often are, and many an actor has been mightily put off at the dress rehearsal to find that he hasn't nearly as much room to move once the real furniture is in position, and that some moves may even have to be altered. The director can help by constantly reminding the cast of the problem, in just the same way as he will warn his actors regularly if their rehearsal acting area is very much smaller than the stage on which they will be performing.

Running the Rehearsal

The very first rehearsal, if you can afford the time to do it, should be a complete read-through of the play, probably preceded by comments from the director, who will want to say something about the way he sees the play, the essential style that he will be looking for, the biggest problems, and a word for each of the cast about their characters. Even if you don't have a read-through (and it is worth doing if only because it ensures that the cast will at least once be aware of those parts of the play in which they themselves do not appear), the director should certainly spend some time in talking about the play and the characters. The sooner the cast know his intentions the better, and the easier later rehearsals will be. There may be a certain amount of discussion—one of your actors may see difficulties in his part or have a very different conception of it from your own. Such arguments should always be encouraged rather than stamped on—again, the sooner problems or disagreements can be brought to light and settled the better.

The director must of course describe and explain the set, though he may prefer to do this when he begins blocking—that is, telling the cast their moves and actions. When setting the stage for rehearsals, as well as using whatever is available to represent the furniture, you need indications of entrances, stairs, rostra and so on. If you have a permanent rehearsal venue which is not used by others, you can stick masking tape on the floor to show the position of scenery, furniture, etc.

We move on to the first real rehearsal, which will normally be spent in blocking. Don't try to do this in one solid stream of instructions at the beginning, but let the cast walk through the scene or act, reading their parts, and tell them of each move as it comes along, making sure that they write the various directions in their copies.

Once you have finished blocking one act, do not be tempted to go on to the next. It is much better to go back over what you have already done, seeing if the actors remember all that you have said, and gently correcting them if they do not.

Generally speaking, it is not possible to pay much attention to characterization or the way lines are said at the blocking rehearsal. Actors cannot take in too much at one time, and will have quite enough to do with sorting out where the exits are, when they come on and go off, when they cross the stage or sit, and so on.

You may feel it necessary to leave certain movements to a later stage. For instance, in the last scene of *Angels in Love* there is a very complex series of movements involving tea-cups being passed backwards and forwards among the cast, and you might not block it in detail until the actors can dispense with their books and have their hands free for the necessary actions. But if you do delay anything in that way, make the cast aware that there is important work to be done at that point, and be sure that they know what their positions will be at the end of the piece of action concerned.

In the early days of rehearsals the director will probably interrupt the actors constantly, suggesting different inflexions, perhaps explaining the interpretation of the lines that he wants, asking for variations in speed or pace or tone. This can be a very time-consuming business, and it is wise not to attempt to do too much at each rehearsal, and always to leave time to have a second run-through of the act the same evening. Amateur actors very often seem to use the first run-through as a warming-up period, and only halfway through the rehearsal do they give the job in hand their full concentration. This is not, I think, deliberate and perverse—it is simply that for most of them there is a certain amount of difficulty in throwing off whatever has concerned them during the day and getting down to the work (for it is work, and very often hard work) of the rehearsals. Why, you may ask, do they not have the same difficulty when it comes to the performances? Well, sometimes they do, and it is not just nerves but also a lack of concentration which leads to sub-standard performances. On the whole, however, the sense of excitement and the release of adrenalin lend an urgency to the performances which is not there at rehearsals.

Again remember that no one can grasp too much at one time, and beware of giving an actor so many directions and suggestions that he cannot remember them all. Start with the broadest of comments, and keep the finer points until a later rehearsal, by which time the actor may have cured the fault in question without any help from you.

Have a notebook in which you can scribble comments as the rehearsal progresses, so that you don't have to keep stopping the action. It is sometimes difficult to write intelligible reminders to yourself when all your attention is engaged in listening and watching, and if you can find time to put the name or initial of the character concerned, it may save you from wondering exactly what you meant when you come to give your notes—that is to say, your comments and instructions—at the end of a section of the play.

As the rehearsals continue, the director will probably interrupt far less often, and will give his notes in batches, stopping the play perhaps after a character's exit or at some other apparently natural break, or if something has gone wildly wrong. He will have to decide whether simply to point out to an actor that something was not quite right and then to proceed with the rest of the scene, or whether to go back to rehearse again the bit that he wants done differently. It is usually wise to go back, because it fixes the change in the actor's mind, but beware of doing so again and again—the average amateur actor has a low tolerance for boredom, and will soon lose interest in repetitions, which are also quite likely to result in other actors starting to get things wrong. Watch for the point the next time you go through the scene, and if necessary repeat it again then once or twice, but no more.

Towards the end of rehearsals, things may be going pretty well, but you will almost certainly feel that the play is moving much too slowly—not necessarily because the actors are uncertain of their lines, or even slow in picking up cues, but because of a sort of deliberation in their manner. Perhaps they are all trying to make the most of their parts. Get the whip out, and make them speed up. Tell them you need to cut at least five minutes' running-time from each act. The result may be a bit of a gabble, and the cast will certainly slow down again to some extent in the performance, but with luck they will not go back to their earlier snail's pace, especially if they realize that the extra speed heightens the drama.

The Director's Relationship with the Actors

The director's problem is that an amateur cast is made up of such different people, taking part for pleasure, and very rarely can any of them be sacked. He needs to be psychologist, friend, kid-glove specialist, and still strong enough to impose his will.

Some actors respond best to the gentlest of handling, others will need to be bullied; some will need only the merest hint of a characterization, while others will have to have everything spelt out in great detail; some will give much the same performances at the first rehearsal and on the last night, whereas others will build up their parts very slowly.

The actor who does not develop during rehearsals will not necessarily give a bad performance. Indeed, one of the best amateur actors I ever worked with was of this type. He would come to the first rehearsal word perfect, would make only the minimum of alterations to the way he played the part if the director particularly asked him to change, and though he was a good enough actor to have got the characterization right in the first place and to respond to the rest of the cast and raise the intensity of his own portrayal or react in some other subtle way to his fellow actors or to the audience, basically the performance was the same as at that first rehearsal.

I think the developing actor is much to be preferred. You can spot him quite easily—you will notice the experiments he tries and the changes he makes at each rehearsal. If you criticize him too firmly, you may stifle his imagination, and the best approach is to give him latitude at first. Later, if his interpretation seems entirely wrong to you, discuss it with him and try to lead him back to what you want.

Some of the cast may be inexperienced, and the director will have to teach them the rudiments of acting. Like all teachers, he will need not only a sound base of knowledge, but a great deal of patience.

Yet another breed of actor is the one who will not give of his best until he has an audience to spur him on. Such people are often difficult to work with, and seem very selfish, for their refusal to Give Their All at a rehearsal may be very off-putting to the rest of the cast, who are putting everything into it. The trouble is that this kind of actor cannot really help it. He gets his adrenalin only when it's for real, and though the director may try asking him to imagine that he, the director, is an audience of a hundred people or more, challenging him to use his imagination in that way, it probably won't help much.

Then there is the actor who finds it very difficult to 'give' much simply because he is too shy and fears being laughed at if he 'emotes'. Try asking him to over-act, to make it deliberately ridiculous. It is usually easier to cut down on hamminess than to lift up from nothing.

Since the director spends so much of his time being critical, he must remember also always to give praise when it is due, and often when it isn't. I have found it worthwhile too, if it seems that I am criticizing one member of the cast to the exclusion of the others (usually because he is not up to the standard of the rest), to find fault with at least one of the others, even if it is not deserved, and have explained in advance to the unfairly criticized actor that I am doing it solely in order to prevent the below-standard player from feeling that he is being 'got at'.

Of course, you must be aware of an individual actor's feelings. If it is plain that the actor is really trying, but having difficulties of some sort, encouragement will achieve more than reading the riot act. And there are always rehearsals when the most reliable members of the cast have an off day—perhaps they are tired, or worried about family or business matters, or just not in the mood. Provided it happens only rarely, the director should treat them gently, especially if, as is often the case, he can see that the actor is worried by his own failings.

Rehearsal Problems

The director needs to have a great deal of patience, particularly at the beginning of the rehearsal before the actors have really begun to concentrate on what they are doing. Actors forget what they have been told, and go on forgetting, and they will stumble over the same lines at rehearsal after rehearsal. When off stage they chat to others, not only distracting those who are trying to rehearse, but often forgetting their own entrances. The director may also have to deal with fits of the giggles from his cast, back-seat drivers giving him suggestions, temperament from his stars, and problems arising from the personal relationships of the players. Questions of discipline are always difficult to resolve, because it has to be remembered that amateurs take part in plays to enjoy themselves and as a form of relaxation. Discipline must be applied, but it should not be too harsh.

Let us look at some of the problems mentioned above.

Giggling. To call your actors to order as soon as they are afflicted with the giggles in the early days of rehearsal will probably produce a slightly sour atmosphere. Let them have their giggles. After a while they will probably die away. If they don't, then calmly and firmly say, 'Come on, let's be serious,' and that will probably do the trick. If the trouble goes on, you can be a little testy.

Forgetful actors. Calm, patient reminders will probably be more effective than anger, but if you are driven by constant repetition to a show of fury, let it be brief and temper it as soon as you can by a compensating display of good humour. Don't ever let the cast see you rattled. A calm director is a great asset to the actors, who will subconsciously see him as the rock on which the production is built.

Talking off stage. This must be taboo, and should be stamped on firmly, but again calmly. It is a good idea to have a tea or coffee break part way through the rehearsal, if that can be managed and you can spare the time, because it gives the actors and others time for a little socializing, which is part of the fun of amateur dramatics. But don't let the break go on too long.

Temperament.   This must be dealt with extremely firmly, but it can be very difficult, because the amateur director usually lacks the ultimate sanction of replacing the actor concerned. I would suggest that he should say something to the effect of, 'We don't have temperament in this society. If you have a complaint to make, let's discuss it now, and see if we can put right whatever it is that's wrong.' If that does not work, and in an extreme case, I would call an end to the rehearsal there and then, and hope that the offender would be shamed into better behaviour next time.

Back-seat drivers.   It can be infuriating to find that as well as yourself you have half a dozen other would-be directors all trying to put their oar in. Don't let them interrupt proceedings, but when you come to a time for giving notes, do ask if anyone has any comments or suggestions to make, and then listen to them, refuse firmly but politely those that you don't like, and be prepared to accept gratefully any good ideas which may come.

When to Lose your Temper

Of course, the answer is never. But there is usually a point in any production when the director needs to jolt the cast, usually two or three weeks before the first performance, when some of them are still very far from word perfect and perhaps at fault in other ways. Now is the time to work up a certain amount of anger and let fly. Keep it general, avoiding personalities, so that you are talking to the whole cast and not just to the offenders—the innocent will be well aware of those you're really getting at. Tell them how badly they're behaving, how hopeless it makes your job, remind them that they expect an audience to pay to see the play, and that they owe it to themselves to do their best. Then let your anger die away, and turn your criticisms into an appeal to do better on the next run-through. They will listen glumly, perhaps angrily, but when they do the scene again they will probably make a better showing of it, and you should be careful then to thank them and praise them for their efforts.

This all sounds like a very deliberate ploy, and you may wonder whether it will be effective if your actors happen to have read this book and seen this piece of advice. Well, yes, it is a deliberate ploy, but since you will not use it, I hope, unless your strictures will be fully justified, it will still be effective—especially if you act it well!

The Difficult Actor

What do you do if part way through rehearsals you find that one of your cast is impossible? Perhaps he queries every line, arguing about interpretation, or wants to change every move that you have given him, perhaps he makes no effort to learn his lines and remember anything you tell him, or perhaps he misses rehearsals and is consistently late for those he attends—in short, he's a pain.

There are nearly always, in my experience, two additional difficulties in such cases: the impossible actor is a personal friend, or is in a position to cause considerable damage to the group if offended, or both. Besides which, it usually transpires that there is no one who could take over his part even if you had the courage to get rid of him.

If a replacement is available, you have a straightforward choice. If not, then all you can do is to have a serious talk with the actor concerned, and if that fails, try an open discussion with the cast present, which will probably be very unpleasant, but if the others in the play support you, you may bring home to the offender the error of his ways. Keep the society's executive committee informed of your problem. Try not to admit defeat by resigning. Ask yourself whether you yourself may be to blame as much as the actor.

You must of course take it seriously if an actor is very unhappy about something you want him to do, or if perhaps he asks if he can introduce a new move or sit at a different point, or something of that sort. Often you will be able to accept the change; if you can't, explain why you want to stick to your original plan, but keep the discussion short. If it is plain that you are willing to listen, especially the first time that a query is raised, your co-operative attitude may prevent the actor from becoming 'difficult' as time goes on.

Absentees

One of the director's constant headaches is that he will very rarely have every member of the cast present at all rehearsals. Actors fall ill, or have other commitments, and the director must simply resign himself to absences. He should always be informed of them, through the stage manager, in advance.

If some members of the cast are missing, he should not read in the parts himself. Get the prompter to read them from the side, or preferably ask the stage manager and anyone else available to read and make the moves on the stage. Do avoid, however, any attempt to get these 'understudies' to move into exactly the right positions or waste time telling them how to say lines—they are not in fact understudies, but simply bodies reading the lines. If they *are* understudies, that is different— and so too is your society, because the majority of amateurs have enough difficulty in filling the cast, without thinking about duplicating it.

Don't Just Tell—Show

When I want to alter the way an actor does something, whether it is a move or the way he says a line, I am a great believer in showing him. Go up on the stage, or on to the stage area, and demonstrate what you want, or say the line the way you want it said. It is much more effective than any amount of verbiage about the point. The only problem is that you must be careful not to show him so well that you give him an inferiority complex. Show him the *idea* rather than the exact thing. Paraphrase the words. Say, 'Try something like this—but do it in your own way, of course,' rather than giving a firm instruction to 'Do this.'

Always Have an Answer

When members of the cast ask you questions about the play, their characters, moves, the interpretation of certain lines, and so on, it is essential, I think, to answer firmly and quickly. Nothing destroys a cast's confidence in the director more swiftly than if he constantly hums and haws. You can get away with saying, 'I don't know. I'll tell you at the next rehearsal,' (a promise you must keep, so make a note about it), but it's better to give a firm answer. If you have second thoughts, keep them until the next rehearsal. Obviously you mustn't keep chopping and changing, and the sooner you make a final decision the better.

Properties at Rehearsals

One of the reasons that books need to be dispensed with as soon as possible is that it is only then that the cast can start practising with properties. Almost certainly the props at rehearsals will not be those you have for the performances, but anything of approximately the right size and shape will do. The point is not only to get the actors used to the props, but to cope with the difficulties that frequently arise because of the lack of stage directions about properties in the acting edition. 'Pours himself a drink,' it says, or 'She hands him the letter,' but it doesn't tell him where or when to put the glass or the letter down. Is he meant to hold on to it until the end of the scene, and if not, when can he move without attracting undue attention and will it upset the moves previously arranged? Problems of this kind are usually sorted out easily enough, but you may not even be aware that there is a difficulty until you have the relevant prop at rehearsals.

Inaudibility

Most amateur casts seem to include some actors who find great difficulty in projecting their voices sufficiently to be fully audible. Even if you are rehearsing in a private house, you can usually tell those who won't be heard. Keep reminding them to speak up. If you are rehearsing on the stage on which you will perform, spend some time at the back of the hall, making sure that you can hear. If you can't, let the actors know. I have found that instead of calling, 'Can't hear' from the back of the hall, it is more effective to pick up the inaudible lines. Let us suppose that a character on stage has to say, 'She was wearing a green hat.' If it is inaudible, I will shout, 'What was she wearing?' 'A green hat,' the actor shouts back. 'Yes,' I say. 'I can hear that. Let me hear it when you say the line.'

Crowd Scenes

If your play involves crowd scenes, you will probably not call the crowd to all rehearsals, bringing them in only at a later stage. At that point it is worth holding one rehearsal solely for them.

Amateur crowds frequently suffer from two defects: they have no individuality and they tend to act and move and stand woodenly, suddenly bursting into life when called upon to react in some obvious way. One of the reasons for this, I feel, is that directors do not always take enough trouble to explain to them who they are, what is going on in the play and their part in it, and to suggest that they should each try to think up a character for themselves. Some caution is needed, for the characterizations in the crowd must not be so strong that they attract the audience's attention away from the main action.

In order to get a crowd behaving apparently naturally, it is probably best to divide them into groups at the rehearsal and work out their moves and reactions in small batches, even individually. Make sure that they know where the principal actors will be standing and moving. Rehearse their entrances and exits, and ensure that they clear the backstage area as soon as possible—there is nothing like a crowd of extras for getting in the way of the stage staff.

Of course, it is traditional that a crowd should say, 'rhubarb'. This word, spoken quietly by a number of people, can give the effect of a general murmuring, but it can equally become quite clear to the audience that it is exactly that which is being said. It is much, much better to work out suitable lines for individual members of the crowd to speak. Ask them to do this for themselves, and they will usually start off well but dry up very quickly, so the director should consider writing appropriate lines for them himself.

Chorus Speaking

I think chorus speaking is difficult enough for professionals, and amateurs are rarely successful with it, especially if any members of the chorus are uncertain of their lines. If you have a chorus, insist that they learn their words with perfect accuracy and fluency. Appoint the actor with the most experience and a good voice as leader, and make the others listen to him and learn the rhythms with which he speaks the lines. Then rehearse and rehearse to make sure you get unity of diction. If your chorus speaks perfectly in time, they will be audible; if only slightly out of synchronization, the sound will be con-. fused. Beware of your players, in their efforts to be distinct, over-elocuting, particularly in verse plays.

Other Rehearsal Activities

If you have the time, and you would need more rehearsals than those shown in the schedule at the beginning of this chapter, you might like to try some other rehearsal ideas. Improvisation, for instance. Actors often seem to have no idea that their characters have any life apart from that which is seen during the play. The more they know of their characters' backgrounds, the stronger their interpretations are likely to be, so you could try getting them to improvise what happens, say, immediately before the play begins. What are all the people in the play doing half an hour previously? It may be that at first you will not get much response, but usually at least one member of the cast will find his imagination stimulated by this question, and once he starts the others will probably follow.

Another kind of improvisation which can be helpful in setting the mood of the play is to ask the cast at a fairly early stage, once they have a really good idea of what happens in each scene, to put their books down and act the play in their own words. There are, however, fairly obvious dangers in this, and it should probably be tried only with experienced actors.

Or you might try a variation of the game played at the beginning of Act Two of *Hay Fever*, asking your actors to perform various actions in the manner of the characters they are playing.

Something else which can be very interesting is to tape a rehearsal, if you have the equipment available, and then play it back to the cast. Hearing themselves say the lines often reveals to them faults which you have been trying in vain to correct.

Pity the Poor Director

Sometimes the director finds his work very dispiriting. The cast hasn't learnt the lines, he never has all of them at rehearsal, he has just been told that he can't have the furniture he wants, the set is quite the wrong colour, and he doesn't believe the show will ever be ready to go on. However worried he may be, he must somehow maintain his enthusiasm and belief in ultimate success.

THE STAGE MANAGER

The stage manager is really the assistant director, and he has a great many duties. He should note all the director's instructions in his copy of the play—moves, pauses, emphases, business, lighting changes, sound effects, and so on. Two pages before a character is due to make an entrance, a warning should be marked so that the call boy (if he has one) can be sent to fetch the actor, and half a page before lighting and sound cues an indication should be made, so that at that point he will warn the lighting or sound director to stand by.

He should attend all rehearsals, arriving a few minutes early so that he can mark out the acting area and arrange the furniture. He should be the person who knows whether any member of the cast is unavoidably absent, and who checks up on anyone who is missing unexpectedly, and he will maintain off-stage discipline during rehearsals. He will watch the rehearsal carefully to see that all the instructions the director has given previously are being carried out, and will point out any mistakes in them. He will also probably be responsible at early rehearsals for simulating any necessary sound effects (a job which may later be taken over by the prompter), and will 'read in' for absentees. If the director is absent or involved in discussions with other members of the production team, he will take the rehearsal, at which he will continue to carry out the director's intentions rather than introducing any ideas of his own.

It is an interesting job, though not a particularly creative one. A good stage manager is invaluable. The director cannot do his job properly if he is constantly looking at the script to see if the lines are correct, nor if he is distracted by the player who can't remember where he is supposed to be at a given point in the scene. He must watch the total effect, and he must listen. Of course he has to be aware of the trees, but he must be able to see the wood too, and it is much more difficult to do so without the freedom from bothering with mechanical details that the stage manager and the prompter can give him.

The stage manager will often have other duties too. It is a matter of choice whether he or the producer makes arrangements to book rehearsal venues, but it is certainly the stage manager who should see that the place is clean, tidy and locked up when everyone leaves, and equally he should be the last to leave the theatre or the hall after performances, having made sure of the same things.

The stage manager will be in total control of the dress rehearsals and the performances. It is he who will send the curtain up, which of course he will not do without first checking that all the beginners (the actors who appear at the beginning of the scene or soon after) are ready, and that the stage is properly set, with all furniture and properties in their correct positions. He will cue in lighting and sound, and will probably act as call boy if he has no one to do the job for him. He will bring the curtain down at the end of each scene or act. At the dress rehearsal he will time the acts so that he can tell the front-of-house manager when the intervals will come.

The stage manager will need a base behind the scenes, out of the way of entrances and exits and scene changes, but from which he can see what is going on and control all that has to be controlled. If possible, he should establish from the time that rehearsals begin exactly where this base will be.

THE PROMPTER

Prompting is a difficult, boring and unrewarding job, usually undertaken by women, partly because the female voice is often clearer than a man's. Few actors ever remember to thank her for getting them out of their difficulties. She must concentrate on her copy of the play at all times, following every word, ready to step in when needed, and this is really not as easy as it might sound, for even the most brilliant of plays can become dull when you read it over and over and over again, without the fun of acting any of the parts.

The prompter should attend all rehearsals, or at least all of them from the time that the actors begin to manage without their scripts. It is essential that she should not only be familiar with the play, but also with the way the actors perform it—a change of intonation may be a sign that the actor is running into trouble and will soon need a prompt. She should mark all pauses very clearly, for there are few things an actor dislikes more than being given a prompt which he doesn't need in the middle of his dramatic pause. Of course, if he's added a new pause in the excitement of performance, he has only himself to blame.

The prompter should also mark any passages which have proved particularly sticky during rehearsals, so as to pay special attention to them during the performances. Since the actor in need of a prompt wants to be given the key words at the beginning of the line, she might also consider marking such words. But nothing she can do can really prepare her for the emergency—an actor can easily dry in performance on lines that he has said perfectly from the very first rehearsal. The prompter has to be ready for anything.

A good prompter will learn the various ways in which members of the cast show that they are in trouble. She should be on the look out for the glazed eye, the nervous movement. She should also be aware of which members of the cast, if any, prefer to improvise their way out of difficulty—and whether she can trust them to do so satisfactorily.

A crisis can arise when, without a pause, the actors leave out some lines, or a whole page of script, or even jump from one act into another. In such cases, unless the omitted lines are few and the cut is of little importance, the prompter must interrupt firmly and try to bring the actors back to the point at which they went wrong.

The worst difficulty is when the play comes to a halt because some action has not been performed or because of the absence of a sound rather than a line. I remember a play in which an actress had to cough, though she did not speak. The subsequent dialogue was about her heavy smoking. Without the cough the play could not continue. When she forgot her 'line', the prompter coughed. What else could she do? The silence continued. The prompter coughed again, louder. The actress still did not pick it up, no doubt thinking what a nasty cold the prompter had. At her wits' end, the prompter bellowed, 'Cough!', and at last the actress remembered and the play went on. The audience thought it was the funniest line of the evening.

For the performances the prompter should arm herself with a torch with a dimmed light (tape tissue paper over the lens), so that she can follow the script even if the lighting on stage is very dim. The prompter traditionally takes a position behind the proscenium arch downstage left (hence the left and right sides of the stage are sometimes known as 'P.' and 'O.P.'—'Prompt' and 'Opposite Prompt')—but there is no reason why this should be followed if it is more convenient for her to be seated elsewhere. She should, if possible, have a clear view of the stage and the actors, but of course must not obstruct entrances.

When giving a prompt there are two cardinal rules: to be audible (better for the audience to be aware of the intervention than for the actor not to hear), and to give the actor enough of the forgotten line for him to recognize it, prompting with a phrase rather than a single word.

THE ACTOR

The actor's job at rehearsals is quite simple—he must work hard to perfect his performance, help others to realize theirs, and carry out the director's intentions.

Inform the stage manager if you will be unavoidably absent from a rehearsal or late arriving. If you have problems with your part, let the director know and discuss them with him, but don't argue unnecessarily or incessantly. Always bring a pencil with you, and mark your script with moves or other directions the director gives you. Don't be temperamental. Don't rely on rehearsals for learning your lines—it helps, of course, especially to hear your cues said by those who will actually be saying them, but you should learn your part between rehearsals. Don't distract others in the cast.

THE FINAL REHEARSALS

The Staging Rehearsal

Prior to the first dress rehearsal it is usually a good idea to have an evening without the cast when scene changes, lighting and sound effects, and any other elements of the staging are rehearsed. If the set is the same throughout, this may not be necessary, but if there are several changes of scene and furniture and lighting it will be essential.

For scene changes the stage director will have to work out which stage hands will move which flats or pieces of furniture and in which order so as to achieve a smooth change, and the lighting director will have to prepare everything for his new lighting schemes. Indeed, this may be the only occasion when the lights themselves can be set up and cued.

This is also the opportunity to rehearse the curtains—that is to say, the precise moment and the speed at which they will be opened or closed or raised or lowered at the beginning and end of each scene. The mood of the scene will dictate the speed. Generally, but by no means always, comedies demand faster curtains than serious dramas, but it depends on the closing lines of the scene and their effect on the characters on stage.

The Dress Rehearsal

The dress rehearsal(s) (preferably in the plural) should be exactly like a performance, with all scenery, furniture, lighting, costumes, properties, and so on.

The play should not stop unless something goes disastrously wrong, and the director should only interrupt if absolutely necessary, giving his notes either at the end of an act or at the end of the whole play.

Before the dress rehearsal begins, he may ask the cast to come on stage, with the appropriate lighting on, so that he can see and approve or disapprove their costumes and make-up.

He should ask the cast to familiarize themselves with the scenery and furniture, and in particular to make sure that they know how doors open and close. They should also be made aware of the lay-out backstage, so that they do not trip over braces, know exactly how to get from one side of the stage to the other, and don't get in anybody's way. If, as sometimes happens, this is the first rehearsal actually on the stage or if the company is performing in a strange theatre or hall, the director may also suggest to the cast that they should try out their voices.

It may be a good idea, provided it does not diminish ticket sales, to have an audience present at one or both of the dress rehearsals. Some societies will allow the cast's friends and relations to come, or may invite a local old people's home to send a group to watch. It is particularly useful to have an audience if you are presenting a comedy, for even though a handful of people find it much more difficult to laugh than a full house does, at least you may get some titters which the cast will be pleased to hear.

Most amateur companies are firmly wedded to the old saw that a bad dress rehearsal means a good first night, and I have even known groups to be worried if the dress rehearsal goes too well. Of course, it should be as perfect as possible, and everyone should be delighted if it is. A bad dress rehearsal gives no guarantee at all of a good performance, and probably means only that the preparation has been inadequate. Not that one ever expects a flawless dress rehearsal. It is taking place precisely in order that difficulties may be discovered and put right, but it is not the occasion for making changes in the way lines are said, or in movements, or in anything else that should have been settled in ordinary rehearsals earlier.

If the dress rehearsal is in fact disastrous, the director can probably do little other than hope that it will, after all, be 'all right on the night'. Obviously, he will have to point out the things that have gone wrong, but it would be very unwise to berate the cast too strongly. It is much too late to make any radical changes, and the actors need encouragement rather than harsh criticism. However, if he senses very early on that the play is going badly, it may be worth stopping and starting again in the hope that the second attempt will be an improvement.

The Curtain Call

The dress rehearsal will probably be the occasion when the curtain call will be arranged. Most amateurs are at their worst in curtain calls, and the director should give them very firm instructions, and should insist on several practices. It is not only a matter of who comes on from which part of the stage and where they stand, but what they do when they get there. You may bring your cast on in sections—the small parts first, leading up to the principals; you may stand them in a straight line, or you may arrange them to make a scene; you may change them around after the first curtain call so that they are in different positions for the second. But you must also tell them when to bow, how long the bow should last, and, I would suggest, what sort of expressions they should wear. It always seems incongruous to me after a very serious, moving play to see half the cast grinning like Cheshire cats at the curtain call, and equally absurd when after a farce some of them put on rather pained expressions, as if to convey that they have exhausted themselves or that they despise the audience for having laughed so much. So tell them to smile or to be serious, tell them when to bow (usually the best way is to take the timing from the player standing in the centre of the stage—but remember that the timing is not only for when to bow, but also for when to come up out of the bow), and tell them to stay in position when the curtain comes down or closes in case the stage manager decides to open it again for another call.

6

Playing a Part

THE ACTOR'S APPROACH

Responsibilities

The first thing that an amateur actor does when cast in a play and given his copy is to go through it, reading his own part. Some never read scenes in which they do not appear, or read the play as a whole. But it is essential that you should do so. When you act in a play you are a member of a team, joining together in the presentation of the play as a complete entity. You must know what it is about, in order to understand your character's function in it and to be able to help your fellow actors to play their parts effectively. Indeed, before you go on stage, either at rehearsal or in performance, stop and remind yourself exactly what you are going on there to do, and what the playwright's intention is, not only in respect of your own character, but for the whole play, and what part you have to take in that intention.

That may be your first responsibility, but the second is equally important in its different way. If you agree to take part in an amateur production, you should be making a commitment. Since amateur drama enthusiasts seem inevitably to be the kind of people who live busy lives, it may not be possible for you to attend every rehearsal, but you have an obligation to attend as many as you possibly can, to arrive promptly, and to let the stage manager know, with as much notice as possible, if you can't come to a particular rehearsal. I once had someone in my cast who suddenly announced half way through the rehearsals that he hadn't realized exactly when we would be performing the play, and he was sorry, but he would be in America at the time! Check that you will be available for rehearsals and performances before accepting the part.

It is not only a matter of committing yourself to rehearsals. Every amateur director often knows, as clearly as if they had all signed a statement to that effect, that not one of his cast has opened the play since the last rehearsal some days previously. Some actors claim that they can learn their lines only at rehearsal. They are a pain, and it isn't true anyway. Rehearsals certainly help, but most of the work needs to be done at home—not only learning the lines, but thinking about your characterization and studying the play as a whole. 'Work' is of course the key word. Amateur drama is fun, but it also requires solid application, and if you are not prepared to work both at rehearsals—which means concentrating on what you are doing and not spending the whole time chattering to your friends or fooling about in some way—and at home, then you'd better find something else to occupy your spare time (though you will probably discover that whatever else you choose will be equally demanding if it is at all worthwhile).

The Actor's Attitude to the Director

Most directors greatly welcome the approach of those actors in his cast who work on the presentation of the character that they are playing, finding out for themselves how he ticks, trying to produce from the lines on the page a believable, well-rounded person. But it is as well not to settle on your interpretation too firmly in advance of the first rehearsals, for your concept may not agree with that of the director. You have to accept the fact that he is the boss, and it is better to discover early on how he would like the character to be played than to get so far with it that it is difficult for you to change.

If you disagree with him about the characterization, talk about it after the rehearsal rather than during it—a long discussion in the middle of rehearsal wastes time and is very boring for the rest of the cast, and may easily develop into a fairly heated argument. If you are going to have a heated argument, it is better to do so in private.

Be patient with the director, and accept the discipline that he imposes. When he makes you go through part of a scene for the umpteenth time, he is probably as fed up with it as you are, but there is something in it which he feels just must be put right.

It Will Be All Right on the Night

One of the most important things at rehearsals is to be aware of what you are doing. Try to listen to yourself and even to see yourself. Watch your movements. Listen to your voice, and notice whether you are getting a good variety of inflexion, tone, rhythm, speed. Be sensitive to the pace of a scene. Experiment and select. And don't hold back, but give of your best.

Some actors seem during rehearsals to be absolutely wooden, cloth-eared and generally hopeless, and then turn into overnight stars when they have an audience to perform to. I wish they'd realize how difficult they make it for everybody else. Produce a little extra when the audience is there, yes, but try to give as much of a real performance as you can during rehearsals.

In *Acting: A Book for Amateurs*, a book published many years ago, Seymour Hicks wrote, ' "Oh, I can never do it at rehearsal, but when I have the paint on my face and the lights are up and the audience in front of me I feel everything and can do it splendidly." Will you kindly realize that the idea may be a comfortable one but it is utterly ridiculous?' And the great actor Macready said, 'Sir, if you cannot do it in the morning, you cannot do it tonight.'

One of the important reasons for ensuring that your performance is firmly fixed at or near its peak before the performances begin is that acting demands the transmission of the actor's emotions and feelings to the audience. He must therefore have those emotions and feelings strongly enough for them to come across, but at the same time he must remain master of them. An actor who comes to life, as it were, only when there is an audience often may not then be able to exercise control as he should have learnt to do in rehearsal. If you have rehearsed adequately you can make subtle variations in what you do as a result of audience reaction, but without changing the basic framework of your characterization or affecting the intentions of either the playwright or the director.

Learning Your Lines

When Noël Coward was directing a play he used to insist that his cast should be word perfect at the first rehearsal. 'That's all very well for professionals,' you may say. 'They've got nothing else to do all day, and besides it's their job.' True, but that does not excuse those amateurs who put off learning their parts until the very last moment, sometimes even being unsure of them right through to the last performance.

'If I learn it all quickly, I find it so difficult later to make any changes that the director may want in the way I say it.' Nonsense. The sooner you learn your lines, the easier it is to make changes, because you are no longer groping for words, the more help you give to your fellow actors, the more freedom you give to the director actually to direct, and the sooner you can start to use gestures and properties.

The director will probably have told you that he wants scripts to be put down by a certain date. Work out how much of your part you need to commit to memory each day or each week so that at the very least you will be able to meet his deadline. If you can do without your book before then, three cheers for you.

Should you put your book away when you have just a glimmering of the lines, and rely on the prompter? No—that just holds up the rehearsal and irritates everyone else. Keep the book until the lines are reasonably secure.

How to learn your lines is a question that you must answer for yourself. Some do it simply by reading their parts over and over; others find it almost impossible to get the lines into their heads unless they are 'heard' by an obliging member of the family; some like to record their cues on a cassette, leaving gaps for their own words; there are those who swear by reading their parts immediately before going to sleep, or by writing them out in long-hand; and yet others use a kind of photographic memory, summoning up a mental picture of the position of the lines on the printed page and sometimes of the actual words.

Obviously, you have to learn your cues as well as your own lines, so that you know when your speeches come, but there is more to this than simply knowing the two or three words in question. Your lines are a response to what another character in the play has said, or they come from the thoughts of your own character or are your reaction to what is happening at that point in the play. It is very important therefore not to learn your lines and cues in isolation, but to be thoroughly aware of why you are saying a given line, of the thoughts behind the words, and often of the things that you are thinking but not saying.

Not only must you think before you say a line, but continue the thought afterwards, until it is changed by the answer you get or until you have a new thought. In real life we almost always have some idea in our minds before we speak, and it is still there after we have done so.

Try to learn your words accurately. Quite apart from the fact that nothing in the play should be altered without permission, assuming that the play is still in copyright, usually the original is much more effective than your approximation, and a paraphrase may alter the dramatic effect of the line and lose the elusive internal rhythm that well-written plays have. Moreover, you may cause your fellow actors all sorts of problems by giving them the wrong cue.

What is this internal rhythm? It is not usually a question of a definite beat, except perhaps in verse plays. It is more a matter of the phrasing, the length of lines, the emphases. A good playwright chooses the words he uses with the utmost care to tell his story, to delineate his characters and to sound right and have this sense of rhythm. In my experience, the better the play and the playwright, the easier it is to learn the lines and to do so accurately, because one is aware of their rightness—which is another way of saying that they have rhythm.

However well you think you know your part, you should go through it word for word regularly to check that you are not making any variations. If you have an efficient prompter, she will have pulled you up during rehearsals if you go astray, either at the time you make the mistake or when the scene is finished. Even so, having been forced to be accurate while rehearsing, you may feel that the performances give you a chance to improvise, to ad lib, or to depart from the script in some other way. Don't. Your improvisation is unlikely to be as good as you think. In the same way, do not alter anything else, but keep the same expressions, the same gestures, the same movements that you have rehearsed. To alter them may throw your fellow actors and may destroy the delicate balance of a scene for which the director has striven.

Nearly all amateur actors find that there are certain lines which somehow refuse to stick in the memory, or which they consistently paraphrase. I have found it useful to play a variety of tricks in my mind to try to solve this problem. Let us imagine, for instance, that I am having the utmost difficulty in remembering the line, 'Let me tell you what happened.' (Simple enough, you would think, but it is often quite straightforward lines which refuse to stay in one's head.) I might say to myself, using tennis terms, 'Let—first service,' and this apparently childish word association will fix 'let' in my mind. Or suppose I keep saying, 'Let me describe what happened,' which might not matter very much, unless the next line in the play is something like, 'You will tell me nothing,' in which case 'describe' does not give the right cue. To fix 'tell' in my brain, I might say to myself, 'William Tell'. When the line comes in the play, William Tell flashes up on the screen of my mind, and I get the word right.

Another device I have used, especially in a long speech, or one with a series of nouns or adjectives, is to look at the initial letters of the words and then invent a mnemonic for them or remember whether or not they come in alphabetical order, or something of that sort. It sounds quite absurd, but it works for me, and might do so for you.

In desperation you can write a line which you can never remember on your hand with a ballpoint, or, if you have an appropriate costume, on your cuff. Or you can have pieces of paper with your lines on concealed at strategic positions on the set. If you have to spend part of the play seated at a desk or table, you can even have your copy of the play on it. But all these are devices of the last resort, and are really only justified in the case of someone taking over a part at the very last minute. If you do use any of these tricks, please do everything you can to hide your cribs from the audience.

Marking Your Script

Many actors find it useful to underline all their speeches in a play, and some also underline their cues (perhaps in a different colour ink).

At the early rehearsals the director will no doubt give you your moves, and perhaps suggest certain emphases, pauses, and so on. Mark them in your copy, so that you learn them along with the lines. Use signs to indicate various things—an oblique stroke between words, for instance, to signify a brief pause, a double stroke for a longer pause, a curve over the end of one sentence and the beginning of another to join them up, underlining to denote stress, arrows to show moves, abbreviations such as 'XDR', meaning 'cross to down right', and any other markings which you can think up and which will be helpful to you.

Always bring a pencil to rehearsals, so that you can note all this kind of instruction—a pencil rather than a pen, because it makes it so much easier to alter if necessary.

Creating a Character

Learning the lines is of course only part of your job as an actor. You have to create a character. How do you do that? First of all, you have to discover what sort of person you are playing, which means not only reading the play as a whole, but finding out as much as you can about the background of the play, the period, the setting, the position in society that the characters hold, what was happening in the rest of the world at the time. It may also be very helpful to study the life of the author. And look particularly into the background of your own character. What was his life like before the play begins? What will it be like after the play ends? Then let your imagination work on the facts you have gathered.

Peter Barkworth, in his excellent book *About Acting*, says that his favourite quotation on the subject comes from Stanislavsky's *An Actor Prepares*: '. . . remember, for all time, that when you begin to study each role you should first gather all the materials that have any bearing on it, and supplement them with more and more imagination, until you have achieved such a similarity to life that it is easy to believe in what you are doing. In the beginning, forget about your feelings. When the inner conditions are prepared, and right, feelings will come to the surface of their own accord.'

Having decided that you are this or that sort of person, how do you actually reproduce the character in yourself? The lines of the part are there to help you, no doubt, and may demand to be said in a way which is halfway to being a characterization. But you would still need to know how to stand and look and behave and speak. The best way of learning all that is by observation. Listen to people of all kinds in everyday life—notice the rise and fall of their tones, their mannerisms, the stress they put on words—and watch their movements, their gestures, the way they stand and sit and walk. Many professional actors, Alec Guinness, Peggy Ashcroft and Beryl Reid among them, say that the first clue to a characterization comes from the feet. If they know what the character does with his feet, how he walks, they can build the rest on that. Other small actions may give you a clue. If you know how a character eats, brushes his teeth, puts on an overcoat, you will find that you can work out how he does a whole host of other things, including the way he would say his lines.

Almost certainly you will not want to copy a real-life model exactly. It is more likely that you will combine characteristics from a number of people to create your character. Besides, real people have a number of bad habits—such as dropping their voices at the ends of sentences, or putting their hands in front of their mouths while they are speaking—which you will not want to imitate on the stage.

You should also of course draw on your own experiences when you are creating a part, not only for details, but also for moods. The experiences you use need not necessarily be totally parallel to the situation in the play, and if, for instance, you have to play a scene in which you are very sad, it may help to create the right mood by thinking of an occasion in your own life when, for some entirely different reason, you experienced great sadness.

Acting with the body. Just now I mentioned beginning to build a character by discovering how he walks. The whole of the body is vitally important to a characterization, and you must act with every part of you all the time you are on stage.

Take, for example, the expression of anger. You learn to say the lines angrily, but, because you become familiar with them during rehearsals, you may say them with your body in a relaxed position, and the result is unconvincing. When we are angry our bodies are usually tense, we move rapidly with a great sense of purpose, perhaps even violently. The body must reflect the mood as much as the voice does. Or think of playing a timid character—his timidity is apparent in every move he makes, as well as in the tentative way he speaks.

It will help your whole characterization if you decide what kind of body your character has, and don't despair if it is unlike your own. Most slim actors who play Falstaff use padding and careful make-up to give the appearance of being fat, but if you were to see an early rehearsal with a good actor in the part, even if you knew nothing about Falstaff, you would guess that the character was fat, because the actor would be thinking of himself that way and moving as though he were.

Nevertheless, it should be stressed that it is more important to identify with the character's actions and desires rather than try to 'be' him physically. Those actions and desires are always there, and do not come to life only when the character speaks. Acting, characterization, is a continuing process which goes on every minute that you are on stage, whether you are speaking or not. Even if you are quite motionless and silent, your *thoughts* should be in character, and this will be reflected in your expression and in your bodily position.

Developing your Character.   As the rehearsals proceed, your character should grow. As you study the part, you will learn more about the person you are acting, and the character will develop. Experiment, trying different ways of saying the lines, and select those that you will incorporate into the final characterization.

Of course, characters do not exist in isolation. You have to build your relationships to the other people in the play, and to its conflicts and climaxes, and this too will expand your concept of the person you are playing. Incidentally, it is something that you must think of especially in the early scenes when you are establishing your character.

Consistency. It is fairly obvious that if the character you are playing speaks with an accent of some kind, you will have to keep it up all through the play. Remember to maintain any other characteristics—age, lameness, drunkenness, illness—throughout your performance or until a point in the play when you change (which you will probably have to do gradually rather than suddenly). This applies just as much to states of mind as to physical characteristics.

Control. A play is not life itself, but a representation of it. The author has selected from life, and as an actor you have to select too, and make sure that the picture you present is one that suits the play and the playwright's intention. You may not be doing the best of jobs if you immerse yourself *totally* in the character. You must always exercise control, and that means leaving a part of your mind outside the character to observe yourself as you perform. It is this observer-self which allows you to react to the audience and to your fellow actors, to build and develop the character as the play progresses, perhaps adding little touches in the early stages which, though barely noticeable, will give the audience a hint of what is to come. It is this vital part of you which remembers that you are on a stage, and stops you from allowing yourself to be masked, or from talking through a laugh; it tells you how long a pause may be held, it judges the pace. In short, it allows you to control your performance, and it is when the whole cast can exercise not only personal control, but a kind of collective control that the finest teamwork is to be seen. *The Craft of Comedy* by Athene Seyler and Stephen Haggard, which is possibly the best book ever written about the playing of comedy, has a lot of useful things to say about control.

The creation of a character is a work of art in which your aim should be to create dramatic truth, which must not be confused with the truth of real life. One of my favourite stories was told by the late John Bourne, who related how, when adjudicating at a drama festival, he had remarked that two of the characters in a certain play did not look in the least like mother and daughter, as they were supposed to be. Whisperings in the audience made him stop, and he learned that they were mother and daughter in real life. 'I don't care,' he said. 'Real truth is not the same as dramatic truth. Whatever their true, real-life relationship, they didn't achieve dramatic truth by convincing me of it.' I remember too an occasion in a light comedy when a woman was cast in a certain part, despite the fact that she was no actress, because the character in the play was her to the life. It was a disaster. Playing herself, rather than the character, she lacked control and was not funny, though in real life she could be hilarious.

Why didn't that mother and daughter achieve dramatic truth? Probably because they had not worked on the relationship in the play, observing, building, selecting, *controlling*. They may have taken their real-life relationship so much for granted as to believe it would be obvious to the audience, but dramatic truth has to be established, and controlled.

Teamwork

The societies that win drama festivals are nearly always praised by the adjudicator for their teamwork. What does he mean? It is not just a matter of the actors in the play all being of a competent standard and being well rehearsed. It is far more a question of all the actors understanding what the play is about and what the significance of each part in it is, and playing unselfishly in the light of that understanding. Playing unselfishly means letting the actor whose scene it is be the focus of the audience's attention, and not distracting them by doing anything, including fidgeting, which will draw their eyes to you at the wrong moment. It means exercising control, and not trying to make your part bigger than the play demands.

Anything you do on stage which puts your fellow actors off is selfish, and you are likely to have that effect if you make changes from the way the play has been rehearsed. Professional actors sometimes confess that they play tricks on their colleagues during long runs. Amateurs must not do so—if you have to hand someone a written message, let it say what it is meant to say, not have some joke on it. Don't improvise, don't move to an unexpected position, and particularly don't upstage the person whose scene it is so that the actor concerned has to play with his face turned away from the audience.

Above all, teamwork comes from a sense of acting *together* and a special and difficult-to-define kind of stimulation that the actors give each other. They act to each other as well as to the audience, they listen and react and give an intensity of feeling back to each other. And of course the whole team concentrates at all times.

Actors in amateur companies are of different standards, and it is quite usual for some members of the company always to play the leading roles. Those players should, however, be prepared to take on tiny parts if called upon to do so, and then use all their skills to support the rest of the cast without ever lording it over them. That is another manifestation of team-work.

Temperament

Temperament does not of course mean only throwing tantrums. It is also what makes a great artiste. It is sensitivity, and fire, and that magic quality which makes us watch an actor whenever he is on the stage, however small his part, the magnetism which will probably make him a star one day.

Many great actors are also temperamental in the sense of being extremely difficult and demanding to work with, though often they are so only because they are perfectionists. If you are a really great star perhaps you can afford to be difficult and demanding, though I suspect that the greatest of them are also generous and kind and temper their egos with a humility towards their art. On the other hand, every great star is temperamental in the sense of having that inner well-spring which gives them their magic.

The star system does not exist in the amateur theatre—at least, it should not. If you have established a reputation as a brilliant amateur actor in your own locality, nevertheless you must never fall into the trap of thinking that the audience has come to see you. It may be true of your relatives and friends, but even they, whether they are aware of it or not, have come to see a play, not an actor. The play is more important than you are, and the less you think about displaying your own talents and the more you think about presenting the play in the best possible way, the better the whole performance is likely to be. And in the end you will enhance your reputation once again. A selfish actor is almost always a bad actor.

As for temperament and tantrums at rehearsals, that is nothing more or less than sheer bad manners, and if you indulge in such antics the amateur theatre can do without you.

When to Refuse a Part

As I have said, you should be prepared to play any part, however small. The one possible exception is if you feel totally out of sympathy with the part or with the play. Even then, you might try to overcome your antipathy, remembering that you have some responsibilities towards your society. Besides, you may find later that the part is much more rewarding than you had thought and that your first impressions of the play were wrong. Have faith in the people who chose it and cast you.

SPEECH AND MOVEMENT

The Voice

Important though the body is in creating a character, the voice is the medium through which the actor communicates most directly with the audience. One of the first requirements of an actor is that he should be audible. 'Project!' the director cries. He may be talking about your whole performance, wanting you to make it 'big' enough to come across from the stage to the audience, so that they can appreciate fully all the facets of your characterization and your actions, but it is more likely that he will be asking you to make yourself audible to the very back of the hall.

It is not just a question of speaking more loudly, and certainly not of shouting. Except for those rare moments when the text of the play demands it, shouting will only strain your voice and irritate your audience. To project you need to speak clearly and distinctly, giving perhaps a little more attention to the consonants than you would in ordinary, everyday speech, but not making so much of them that you sound unnatural and as though you are 'elocuting'. You must also be careful not to drop your voice at the end of sentences and phrases, so that the words disappear, nor to gabble, running the words together into a mere jumble of sound. And you need to breathe correctly, so that the power of the voice is supplied by air coming up from the diaphragm rather than being produced simply in the throat, and know when to take a breath, especially if you have a long line to say, the breath obviously being taken at a point in the line where there is a natural break, even though it is not always indicated by a comma or any other punctuation mark in the text. In the early days of learning lines it is a good idea to work out where in a long speech you must take breath, and mark your script accordingly.

But none of this is really what the command to 'project' means. What the director is really asking you to do is to throw your voice. That doesn't make it any clearer, so let me try to explain. Put an experienced actor on a stage and ask him to speak, without shouting, so that his voice can be heard at the back of the hall; then ask him to speak in exactly the same tones, but so that he can be heard no farther than halfway to the back; finally ask him to repeat the exercise so that he is audible only to the front rows. He will do it without difficulty, and what he does is called 'throwing the voice'. A stage whisper is indeed a whisper, but a good one has enough projection to let the whole audience hear every word.

How can you learn to do this? It would not be a waste of time for each member of most amateur groups to be given a chance at some time to stand on the stage of your theatre or hall and try the exercise for himself. I don't think it can be taught. It is something you have to experiment with. Stand on the stage and say to yourself, 'I am aiming my voice at halfway down the hall,' or to whatever part of it you want. You will probably feel foolish, but making a fool of oneself is often part of the fun and the work of being an amateur actor, so don't give up. With luck, you will soon master the trick, and once you have it, like riding a bicycle, you don't forget it.

Projecting is not all you have to worry about as far as your voice is concerned. You need to be sure that you have a variety of tone and expression and speed, so that all your sentences do not sound the same. Of course, it isn't always easy to hear yourself as you speak and to know exactly what you are doing with your voice. The director will probably tell you if you don't sound right, but it is helpful to have a tape recording (preferably of an actual rehearsal rather than just of you saying your lines at home) to which you can listen with a very critical ear, as though you were a stranger. Look out for the rise and fall of your voice, the variations in speed, and colour.

Listen too for the desirable contrast between yourself and the other actors, and make sure that you are not catching their voice tones and patterns, which is very easy to do. If everyone speaks with the same kind of inflexions and at the same rate, the result is very monotonous.

You can draw the pattern of your sentences and phrases in a line which follows the rise and fall of your voice, and if you want to you can further refine the drawing by making the line thicker where you lay emphasis on certain words. You could even make a sort of graph, with the tone registered on the upright side and the speed along the base. The point is to make sure that the lines do not repeat the same patterns again and again.

Another problem which particularly affects female actors is the twittering effect that sometimes results if their voices are rather high in pitch. The light soprano voice is not so easy to listen to in speech as the contralto. Cultivate the lower tones, ladies, but beware of doing so with such enthusiasm that you become gruff, and still remember to keep the inflexions rising and falling.

Elocution. One of the dictionary definitions of elocution is 'the art of public speaking as regards delivery, pronunciation, tones and gestures; manner or style of oral delivery'. Often in recent years 'elocution' has been used as a term for over-careful enunciation, which sounds quite unnatural. That kind of speaking is certainly to be avoided, but at the same time the actor has to make himself heard and understood, and to do so needs some of the techniques that elocution can teach, such as the careful sounding of consonants, especially at the end of words, the glottal stop (the tiny pause which prevents the consonant at the end of one word attaching itself to the vowel at the beginning of the next), the elimination of the intrusive 'r' in a phrase like 'the law(r) of libel', avoiding dropping the voice at the end of sentences, and so on.

Accents.   One of the hallmarks of an amateur production all too often is that the play which requires American or regional accents is performed by a cast each member of which seems to come from a different part of the world. Some actors find it much more difficult than others to pick up accents, and to maintain them.

It helps a great deal if the group can find someone with an authentic accent of the kind that they are trying to reproduce and induce that person to read a large part of the play into a tape recorder. The actors will still have to put the expression and variety in, but at least they will be able to hear the dialect pronunciations. If you can't do that, then listen to radio and television presentations set in the appropriate area.

Victor Spinetti once said that the key to speaking in an American accent is to put the stress on the adjective rather than the noun, and to watch for those words like 'cigarette' (accent on first syllable) and 'primarily' (accent on second syllable) where the accented syllable is different in the U.S.A. and in Britain. An American accent is not achieved by speaking through the nose. Mr Spinetti is entirely right in what he says, and I would add to it that there is a different lilt or cadence to American speech, a difference in the tone-patterns. Listen to the actors in American films or on television and you will detect it. Special attention should be paid to vowel sounds— not only the obvious short 'a', but also, for instance, the short 'o' sound in a word like 'John', which in America often becomes more nearly 'Jahn'. And note too that Americans tend not to use the indeterminate 'uh' sound as much as we do when we say, for instance, 'uh ladduh' (a ladder), the American version being likely to be 'ay laddur'.

Vowels are vital in accents. When in *My Fair Lady* Professor Higgins says, 'An Englishman's way of speaking absolutely classifies him—the moment he talks he makes some other Englishman despise him,' he is thinking chiefly about vowels. They are the key to where we come from, as most of us demonstrate in everyday speech. We are usually not conscious of how our vowels sound, and often believe we are sounding them purely when in fact we are pinching them or inflicting some other torture which we probably don't intend. Listen to yourself on a tape recorder if you have any doubts, or even if you don't.

Be very careful if you are using an accent to retain your audibility. One amateur actor I worked with was brilliant at all accents—Yorkshire, Welsh, Irish, American, whatever it was sounded absolutely authentic. The only trouble was that the accent was usually so strong that it was difficult to understand what he was saying.

Attack, Speed and Pace

Directors, and especially adjudicators, will often use these terms.

Attack is perhaps the most difficult to define. I think it really has more to do with firmness of characterization and certainty of direction than with the kind of zip in the production that the word suggests. Attack, or the lack of it, is to be sensed chiefly at the beginning of things—the first words of lines, entrances, the start of a new section of the play. It is to do with coming on to the stage firmly, so that the audience's eyes are drawn to you, and with the vigour that you put into your words, and often with the way you jump in with your line following your cue. It is, in short, to do with being positive, which is why attack can apply even if the character you are playing is supposed to be timid and uncertain, for if you immediately establish that timidity and uncertainty you will be giving attack to your performance.

Speed and pace sound as though they mean the same thing. Not so. Speed refers to the rate at which the words in a speech are delivered—rattled off at a rate of knots, or spoken with slow deliberation, or any variation in between those extremes.

Pace has nothing to do with the speed of the individual words and everything to do with the quickness or slowness with which each character's speeches follow those of the previous speaker. A good pace is usually achieved by picking up cues smartly in this way, and often by overlapping, by which I mean that you begin to say your line before the previous actor has finished his. Obviously you must not do this if the end of the line which is your cue contains words to which you are replying or if its content is of some significance, but if the conversation is comparatively trivial, a certain amount of overlapping will not only lift the pace, but will appear natural. We all interrupt each other, and speak while others are still finishing what they have to say, and we can, for very short periods, listen to and hear more than one person speaking at a time.

The pace does not always need to be fast, and on occasion a play may demand that it should drop considerably, with pauses at the end of speeches. Variety is needed in pace, as in everything else. However, a slow pace is usually effective only if used in moderation and as a contrast, and if the pauses are dictated by the meaning of what the characters say and the thoughts behind their words.

If you are to pick up your cues smartly, you must learn them as well as your own speeches. It really doesn't work to wait until there is a pause, however slight, after the other character stops speaking while you register that this must be where you are to say your next line. The play will sag, and there will be no sense of cut and thrust in the dialogue.

But supposing it's the other person who doesn't come in quickly enough—what can you do then? Not a great deal, but try not to let yourself catch his slow pace. If you keep jumping in sharply, it may result in a very uneven stop-go, stop-go effect, but at least that's better than nothing but stop.

Watch out for places where another character is supposed to interrupt you. Although interrupted speeches are often incomplete in the text, you should know how the line would continue if you were not interrupted, and be prepared to say the rest of the sentence or a part of it if your fellow actor does not cut in as soon as he should.

The Pause

The pause is one of the most effective devices available to the actor, but it needs to be used sparingly and deliberately. It is interesting that an audience can always sense whether a pause is intended or not. If it is intentional and is in the right place, they will often wait patiently and attentively for a long while before it ends. One of the most impressive pauses I have ever seen was in the Chichester Festival Theatre presentation of *The Cherry Orchard* with Claire Bloom. I did not much care for the production, but it had one magical moment almost at the end of the play when the family is about to leave the house, and they were all there, totally still and silent for what seemed like minutes. It was very effective and moving.

Seymour Hicks wrote, 'The value of the pause in acting is priceless, for, get this well into your head, words, important as they are for explanation, comedy or the conveying of poetic thought, can never stir an audience to its depths as does the pain, terror, fury, passion or despair which rises in silence from the heart of a great artist.

'Words are only the lesser part of drama in its higher acting flights. They are necessary only in that they help the audiences to listen to the artist thinking.'

Although one might consider that a little overstated, there is much truth in it. Sir Seymour continued with some advice which is perhaps rather old-fashioned and 'hammy', but nevertheless interesting: 'I have omitted to give you one important rule in discussing pausing. Never do so without beforehand attracting the attention of your audience either by a very definite look, or better still when possible by an exclamation.

'Also remember that if you draw in your breath when saying the word "Oh!" an audience unconsciously does the same, mentally. If, on the other hand, you exhale when saying "Ah!" the spectators will relax with you.'

Pointing

You may be asked to point a line. What it usually means is that you make a slight pause before the key word or words, which results in them being emphasized. For instance, if you say the line, 'Have you been drinking?' with a very brief pause before 'drinking', you have pointed the line. It is a technique which is much used in comedy, where, incidentally, the laugh nearly always comes because of the last word in the line. Alter the order of the words and you will probably lose the laugh.

But pointing is used in all kinds of situations to lend emphasis and thereby to convey a particular meaning. Take the line, 'Have you been seeing this girl?' and think of the different interpretations you get if you point it in various ways: 'Have you been—seeing this girl?' or 'Have you been seeing—this girl?' or 'Have you been seeing this—girl?'

Reacting

It is usually easy enough to react when you have an important part in a scene and what has been said or done affects you, but it is much more difficult if you are simply a silent spectator on the stage. Most people will be able to recall instances in amateur productions when highly dramatic scenes have been going on between two or three characters while the rest of the cast sit or stand on stage in total impassivity, coming to life only when they have something to say and immediately relapsing into wooden-faced stillness once the line has been said. You must react to what is happening, remembering that you are supposed to be hearing it for the very first time.

This does not mean that you should produce a ceaseless series of facial contortions, but you must *listen*, and appear to be listening, and then react to whatever it may be that is startling. Your reaction may be surprise, dismay, amusement, contempt, or even boredom—any kind of emotion demanded by your character's response to the situation. Let me stress again, however, that listening does not mean reacting to every word that is said. We do much of our listening with expressionless faces, but there is all the difference in the world between an expressionless listening face and one that is miles away.

Don't let your eyes wander. If they move away from the person who is speaking, they must do so with a purpose, not casually—perhaps to convey your own emotions or thoughts to the audience, or to glance at something on the stage to which the other person is referring. In many amateur productions the lighting spills over into the first few rows of the audience; don't look at Aunt Mary sitting in the front row, or if you must look in that direction, don't *see* her, don't let yourself be aware that it is Aunt Mary.

Remember too that if there are others on the stage, it may be to them that your reaction is expressed. Let us suppose that Lady Georgina has just been unmasked as her husband's murderer; you, a mere onlooker in the scene, have been listening intently to the detective; when he names Lady Georgina, your features express surprise, and you turn first to your equally silent neighbour on the stage to share your astonishment with him, remembering, of course, to stay in character.

Perform the Play as Though for the First Time

Although you know perfectly well what will happen next in your play, try to pretend with a part of your mind that you do not. If you can succeed in this, it will give a freshness to your part, your reactions will seem more genuine, and the audience will feel that you are sharing with them in a story that has never been told before.

One of the things that is often new to the characters in a play is the room that they enter. If you are playing someone who has not previously seen the room where the play is set, take a quick glance round as you enter. You would do it in real life. When we go into a strange room, we look quickly to see where the furniture is, whether there is anyone else in the room, what the decorations are like, and so on. Don't overdo it, but do remember that you are seeing it for the first time.

Movements

Movements on stage should almost always be very definite (the exception being if you intend to appear unsure or even furtive). Unless you are moving only a few inches, perhaps to get yourself into exactly the right position, don't shuffle or edge your way from one place to another. Move as though you meant it.

The timing of your moves in relation to your speaking of lines is important. Movement before the line is said tends to emphasize the line, and movement after the line to emphasize the movement. To move during the line usually diminishes the effect of both, and to move during someone else's line is almost always distracting, and should never be done unless you are very much the dominant character in the scene and the other character's line is not of great significance.

Turning on the stage should always be done towards the

audience. So, if you are facing stage left and have to turn to stage right, you move so that the audience sees your face rather than the back of your head on the way round. Usually, the simplest way of doing this is to turn by the shortest route. Equally, if you are opening a door stage right, you do so with your upstage, right hand, which for most people is the normal way, but if the door is stage left, then you use your upstage, left hand, which may seem less natural, but looks better.

Turning your back on the audience.   Most amateur actors are taught very early on that to turn your back on the audience is a major sin. Of course, there are times when you can and must break the rule—you can't move upstage backwards, as though from a royal presence—but there are good reasons for its existence. It is not only that you will possibly be inaudible if you are facing away from the audience, since the acoustics where amateurs perform are not always of the best and the scenery tends to muffle sound, but because with your back to them the audience cannot see your face, and particularly your eyes.

After the voice, eyes are our most important means of communication and even at a distance can be very revealing. This, incidentally, is one reason why actors need to control their eyes as much as they control their voices and their bodies when they are acting, for it is remarkable how clearly an audience can tell if you are not looking where you are supposed to be looking, and how easily the eyes betray insincerity.

Most of us also have an ability, admittedly limited, to lip-read, and find it easier to hear and understand someone if we can see their lips moving. If, therefore, you are directed to play a scene or a small part of it with your back to the audience, you must remember to speak particularly clearly and at a slightly higher volume than usual.

It cannot be repeated too often that the audience wants to see your face and your expression as much as possible. If you are upstaged—that is, if you are speaking to an actor who is positioned nearer to the back of the stage than you—it is not necessary to turn to him all the time. You can say some of your lines while facing directly out front, or at least turning only partially towards him. If the scene is more than a few speeches long, you should point out to the director that you are having to play it all upstage. If it is something that has not been rehearsed—an improvised move by your fellow actor, perhaps deliberately to upstage you—you should try to move upstage too, so that you are on the same level as he is.

Make sure they see. Don't look at the floor all the time, or even very much. It isn't usually very interesting, and doing so prevents the audience from seeing your face. If you are facing to the front, although you will not of course gaze rigidly in one direction, you should in general be looking no lower than the heads of the audience in the back row, and if you are acting in a theatre or hall with a balcony, you need to keep your head up even more.

While on the subject of letting the audience see what they want to see, properties might be mentioned. Some props have comparatively little significance in the play, but suppose we are talking of the cigarette case which Algernon produces near the beginning of *The Importance of Being Earnest*—that is a prop of great importance, and the dialogue that follows is devoted to it. Whenever a property is either going to be talked about or is to have a major part in the development of the story, it is essential that the audience should be given a chance to see it clearly.

Something else to bear in mind is the old theatrical adage, 'Tell them you're going to do it, do it, tell them you've done it.' What does this mean? Let us take some examples. You have an important moment when you see something through a window. Before you move, glance towards the window (you've told the audience that you're going to look out of it), then move to the window and gaze out (you're doing it), and finally turn back into the room (you've done it).

Again, suppose you are Mr Collins about to propose to Elizabeth Bennet in the stage version of *Pride and Prejudice*. You bend your knee, but stop, look at the floor with some disgust, and then take a handkerchief from your pocket (telling the audience what you are going to do). You spread it on the floor and kneel delicately on it (doing it). You smile briefly with satisfaction (you have done it) before proceeding to the proposal.

Or you have some surprising news to impart. Before your speech, your expression and attitude reveal your anticipation of the effect it will have. You deliver the line, and then convey the sense that you are thinking, 'There, now! What do you think of that?'

Entrances and Exits

Among the most important moments for actors are their entrances and exits, especially the first entrance. 'Never under-estimate the value of your first entrance in a play,' said Seymour Hicks, 'for the impression you make, be it good or bad, will be lasting.' This is no time for timidity. You have to come on stage firmly and very much in character, so that the audience realizes almost immediately what sort of person you are.

Make sure (with the director's approval, of course) that you are fully visible as soon as possible. Entrances are often partially obscured by furniture, and you need to come out from behind that settee and let the audience see you just as soon as you can.

There are occasions when you will be speaking as you enter, but it is generally better to make your entrance and then speak. Apart from putting the right emphasis on the line, this will give the audience time to take you in.

Exits are often made as you are speaking, or immediately after you have said your 'exit line'. Depending on the import-ance of the line, it may be effective to go off while still speaking, to speak first and then make a long exit, or to move to the door, stop and turn, and then give your line before turning quickly to go off.

What happens when you go off stage, by the way? Do you immediately drop your characterization and revert to your normal self? Perhaps, during the performance, you go back to the dressing-room. If it is the interval, all the cast will be there, and naturally you will not all be so deeply into your characters that you spend the break talking and behaving as they would. But inside yourself you need to keep the characterization going, remembering what you have already done in front of the audience, and thinking about what the character in the play will have been doing while off the stage, so that when you appear again there is a kind of continuity with your previous appearance.

Masking

Masking is what happens when an actor is obscured, usually by one of the other actors, from the audience's view. He is then said to be masked. Undesirable at any time, you should never let it happen to you when you have a line to say, or a piece of business to perform, or if your reaction to what is happening on the stage is of importance.

If your director knows his job, he will have arranged the movements and the grouping so that no one is ever masked for more than a second or two and certainly never when the audience's attention should be on that member of the cast. In a crowd scene, especially on a small stage, some masking may be inevitable, but even then the director should work out the positions so that any member of the crowd with a significant part to play is clearly visible. If, during the rehearsals, you find you are being constantly masked, bring it to the director's notice.

It is more likely that masking will happen accidentally during a performance as a result of one of the other actors moving out of position, perhaps because a piece of furniture is not exactly where it was expected to be, or simply because he has forgotten that he should not be standing in front of you. It is *your* responsibility to get unmasked. Don't tell the offender in an urgent whisper that he's in the wrong place, or push him out of the way. Simply move a pace or two so as to unmask yourself, even if this means altering the position the director gave you, but be careful not to mask anyone else by your move.

On some small stages it is very easy for an actor standing upstage to be masked from a part of the audience by actors who are down right or down left. If you think this is happening, and provided it will not upset anything else, take a step or two downstage.

There are occasions when, although masked, you can't move. You might be an invalid, confined to a chair. You still mustn't hiss instructions at the masker. The answer might be a little ad-libbing. 'Don't stand there,' you might legitimately say. 'I can't see you properly. Move over to the fireplace.'

It is not, by the way, only other actors who mask you. Furniture and props can do it too. I once decided before the first performance of a play I was directing that a little more dressing would help the set, so I put a largish pot plant on a table, forgetting that it would not be very helpful to an actor who would be sitting behind it. When he sat at the table he did nothing about the plant, with the result that we had some remarkable talking foliage in that play. The adjudicator thought it was a rotten idea. If you should ever be masked by a pot plant, the message remains the same: move yourself, or move it.

Speaking personally, I can never understand an actor letting himself be masked. I am much too conceited, and want the audience to see me all the time I am on stage, especially if I am speaking.

Fidgeting

When you have completed a move on the stage, or are just standing, do keep still. Don't shuffle your feet, either when you are speaking or when listening. Fidgeting is very distracting. If you arrange your feet as shown in the following diagram, you will find that you can stand still for quite long periods without feeling discomfort or the need to move.

Gestures

Gestures on stage should be definite and often fairly full-blooded, which usually means extending the arm fully or at least not keeping the elbow tucked firmly into the side. Ideally they should start with the hand moving out from the centre of the body. Once you have made a gesture, hold your arm out long enough to avoid it looking as though you feel that if you leave it there for more than a second someone will bite it.

Gestures should be made whenever possible with the upstage arm if you are standing side on to the audience.

Rehearse your gestures as carefully as you rehearse your words, watching yourself in a mirror, and make sure that they are both in character and meaningful. 'Nothing is more deplorable than a gesture without a motive,' said François Delsarte, the pioneer of expressionism in the theatre.

The timing of gestures is important too. Suppose you have to say, 'Over there,' pointing to the place; there is a subtle difference between pointing first before saying the line, and pointing as you say 'there', and saying the line before pointing. Try it and see.

Be sparing with your gestures. In certain period plays, or perhaps if you are playing a comic character of the Latin race, you may need to use your gestures with great liberality, but generally, as Hamlet says, 'do not saw the air too much with your hand'.

Seymour Hicks again: 'A common fault among beginners is that of making a noisy gesture as they speak a vital line. For instance, they may have to bang a table as they say, "How dare you do that?" If the fist comes down as the line is spoken the words will not be heard and so the reply also will be of no value; therefore make a point of striking the table before you speak, for by attracting the audience's attention by action, the sentence will have a double value.'

Hands

In everyday life most people do not think about their hands or wonder what to do with them. Put someone on a stage, however, and his hands immediately become the most enormous problem to him—and in this case the male pronoun is especially appropriate, for this awkwardness seems to afflict men more acutely than women. In contemporary plays men have trouser pockets where they can bury the obtrusive appendages, but that may be no solution if they are in period costume. In any case, it looks bad to see all the men in the cast with their hands in their pockets throughout the play. It looks equally bad to see players clutching at the furniture, as though they are in need of physical support, though in fact they usually do it only because it keeps the hands occupied.

The real answer is to try to forget the hands, let them hang naturally, and use them only when they need to perform some function or to make a gesture of some kind. But it's easy enough to say that, and it doesn't take away the embarrassed feeling. If you can't persuade yourself to leave your hands alone, you could try clasping them behind your back (the problem is usually acute only when the sufferer is standing up), or folding your arms or putting them akimbo, or putting one hand to the face, holding the elbow with the other hand. There are other possibilities. The important thing is to work them out. Study your non-gestures, as well as your gestures, in front of a looking-glass, timing them to the lines that you say or listen to. Concentrate on what you can do with your hands to add to the scene, and with luck they will cease to be, if you will pardon the splendour of the mixed metaphor, a millstone round your neck.

Mannerisms

Beware of personal mannerisms. Many of us do odd things with our heads, hands and other parts of the body, especially when tensed up in a performance. The director may be shy of telling the actor about such things, because a comment may seem so personal as to be rude. I think it is quite a good idea for the actor to make the first approach, asking the director specifically if he has some mannerism which he should try to correct.

SPECIFIC SITUATIONS

Comedy and Farce

When you play comedy and farce you must do so seriously, and that applies particularly to farce, in which the fun usually depends on the characters taking a ludicrous situation as a matter of life and death. In a highly artificial comedy like *The*

Importance of Being Earnest nearly all the characters fire off strings of epigrams, but even these are delivered seriously and Algernon is the only person in the play who may be allowed to be conscious of his own wit. In most modern comedies the characters are not setting out to be deliberately funny, and though the audience may be convulsed by what they say, the actors remain impassive. One of the worst sins, unless it is strictly within character for you to do so, is to laugh at the funny lines, particularly if they are your own lines. 'Corpsing', as it is called—that is, laughing or giggling on stage when you are not supposed to do so—often has the effect of killing the audience's laughter. It reminds them that you are no more than actors and they lose their concentration on the play.

There are some things you can do if you find it difficult not to laugh. Firstly, say the lines and rehearse the particular part of the play so often that it ceases to be amusing to you. It may still be difficult for you if the audience laughs uproariously at the lines in question or if they laugh at something which you had not expected them to find so comic. It is sometimes possible to turn upstage briefly while you control your twitching lips. If not, at least avoid the eyes of the actors on stage with you—if they are twinkling with suppressed laughter it will be much harder for you to control yourself. You can do this either by looking firmly at some other part of their face, or by altering your focus so that you cannot see their faces clearly and are in fact looking beyond them. It also helps to clamp the back teeth together tightly.

When you are rehearsing you can note the places where you expect an audience reaction, so that in the performance you are ready for the laugh when it comes. Don't, however, be put off if there is no laugh where you had felt sure there would be one, or if there's a great guffaw on a line which had never struck you as funny—audience reaction is very often unpredictable. I worked regularly with a director who, quite rightly acting at rehearsals as the audience, used to go, 'Huh-huh!' on laugh lines in order to get the cast to wait before the next line, to avoid speaking through the laugh. The only trouble was that our audiences didn't always laugh where he had huh-huh'd, and vice versa.

Period Plays

Athene Seyler says in *The Craft of Comedy* that the first
essential is to try to realize the manners of the period. I think
the most effective way of doing this is to consider the costumes
and the furniture.

Until the twentieth century, nobody slouched, chiefly
because their clothes did not allow it (at least from the sixteenth century on) and because their furniture was uncomfort-
able by present standards. Except for the elderly, an upright
carriage was the rule. From the sixteenth century onwards,
both sexes wore restrictive clothing, and of course this applies
particularly to the women who, even in the Regency period of
loose gowns, were well corseted. Corseting in the sixteenth
century was so tight that it resulted in the carriage of the arms
at an angle rather than close to the sides. It is usually easier for
modern women to wear period costumes well than for the
men, who need to remember the peacock quality of their
clothes at least up to the mid-nineteenth century—they were
beautiful and elaborate and were worn with style.

Of course, no woman crossed her legs when sitting until the
twentieth century, and even the men did so with rather less
ease than at present. Don't neglect the use of props—the
handkerchief, the spy-glass, the fan. Study the paintings of the
period to see how people stood and sat.

One of the things that so many amateurs get wrong in period
plays is the way the men bow. The women can usually manage
a reasonable curtsey, but the 'making of a leg', which occurs so
often in seventeenth- and eighteenth-century plays seems to
elude their male partners. The reason is that they tend to put
the right leg forward and bow over it, whereas it is the left leg
which must be moved and to the rear. For the sixteenth century, move the left foot a short distance behind the right, place
the right forearm across the waist, and bow, bending the head
forwards. For the more elaborate bows of the later periods, the
left foot goes a little farther back, and the left knee is then bent,
while the right leg remains straight, thus making 'the leg'. The
head may remain up, looking at the person bowed to, and the
bow may be accompanied by elaborate movements of the right
arm, possibly flourishing a handkerchief.

The ladies, on the other hand, are often at fault in the way they walk. In most period plays small steps are the rule. Athene Seyler says, 'A woman ought to dance as she moves in a seventeenth-century play, to sail in an eighteenth-century one, to swim in a nineteenth-century dress (with tiny even steps under a crinoline or bustle), and to stride in the twentieth century.'

Eating and Drinking

Anyone who has to eat on stage needs to rehearse it assiduously and well in advance of the dress rehearsal. You need to time exactly the moments when you will put something in your mouth, leaving yourself the opportunity to chew and swallow before your next line. Always take very small bites or forkfuls, especially if the food you have to eat is dry and crumby or chewy. At the same time, if you are supposed to be having a large meal, make an effort to look as though you are eating a lot—we must all have seen amateur productions in which a character, supposedly as hungry as a wolf, takes two or three mouthfuls of the food and then announces himself full to bursting.

The food supplied should always be easy to eat. Whatever you are given, concentrate on the things which slip down most easily.

Take a breath before drinking—it will help you not to choke. If your wine cup or beer mug is in fact empty, remember to swallow as though you have actually drunk something.

Kissing

Many amateurs find it embarrassing if they are called upon to kiss passionately in a play, and will often try not to rehearse the kiss properly until the dress rehearsal. If you are wise, you will rehearse it fully as soon as you both can put your scripts down. You do not in any case always have to kiss full on the lips, especially if you can turn so that one of you is upstage of the other. The main point, however, is for the couple to remember that they are acting, and that the kiss means nothing in the personal sense (unless they want it to, of course, in which event as always control must be exercised!).

You must watch out for the effect that a close embrace may have on make-up, trying to avoid unfortunate smudging or getting the stuff on clothes. I once contrived to leave half of my moustache (false, I hasten to add) clinging to a lady's face!

One of the frequent faults shown by amateurs who are kissing on stage is that their feet are in the wrong position. A kiss does not look passionate if the participants are standing eighteen inches away from each other, so that they have to lean forwards and their bodies have no contact. Make sure that your feet and hers are close together, and even if the kiss itself is fairly perfunctory, the general effect will be much better. When you break from the kiss, for heaven's sake don't have a 'thank goodness that's over' look on your face—unless you are interrupted, most embraces will end slowly and affectionately.

Crying

Some actors, especially women, can cry to order, and it is very effective for the audience to see real tears coursing down your cheeks. Edith Evans used to say that she made herself cry by thinking of something very sad in her real life. If you can't persuade the tears to come, one trick is to put your hand to your mouth, deposit a little saliva on your finger and then, when you brush away your 'tears' the saliva will leave an affecting dampness on your cheeks.

Remember that crying doesn't usually stop abruptly, even if you are suddenly feeling quite cheerful, and a few sniffs and dabbings at the eyes should continue after you have finished crying.

Calling Off Stage

If you have to shout or call to someone off-stage, you can give the effect that they are a long way off by lengthening the vowel sounds.

Smoking

This is a problem only for non-smokers. You may be able to cut the smoking. If not, you will have to rehearse it regularly and learn how to light the cigarette, cigar or pipe, how to hold it, and how to avoid choking (mainly by taking very small puffs). Once the thing is lit, you can probably get away with holding it for most of the time, rather than smoking it feverishly.

You should time the draws on your cigarette so that you don't find yourself speaking with a mouthful of smoke, which looks unpleasant and can make you cough. For the same reason, it is best not to inhale.

Talking on the Telephone

The standard amateur fault in a telephone conversation is not pausing long enough to allow the supposed person on the other end to say whatever he is supposed to be saying. If you have to speak on the telephone in the play, it is worth writing out what the other person would be saying and learning it. Say your line, and then listen in your mind to the reply before giving your next line. But mix in a little art. If you pause for exactly the time it would take for the reply to come to you, it may be boring for the audience, so speed it up, especially if you are supposed to be listening to a long message of some kind. You may be able to keep the audience's interest during it by nodding or shaking your head or by some other business which will reveal something of the nature of the call and of your character.

Don't hide your mouth with the telephone, but keep the mouth-piece below your chin.

Drunkenness

Playing a drunk is easy—you simply stagger about the stage and slur your words. The only trouble with that is that your words won't be understood and your staggering will almost certainly look wildly exaggerated. Very few drunk parts involve that stage of inebriation, which is near to incapability. More often you should be at the point when the person who has drunk too much knows it and is trying to hide it or overcome it, which he does by a careful deliberation in his movements and speech. He may sway a little, his eyes may be slightly glazed, he may find difficulty in focusing, and certain words may be hard to say, but all these things should be done in moderation.

Age

It often happens in amateur drama that you are called upon to take the part of someone very much older than yourself. All too frequently young actors playing the part of someone in their sixties or older will adopt a quavery voice and shuffle about the stage, bent almost double, with the aid of a stick. Well, maybe it's right for the elderly person in the play in question, but it's often wrong. Observe people you know of that age. You will find that in most cases they may not stand as straight as in their youth, their shoulders may be a little bowed, their movements will tend to be slower, and they will almost certainly sit and get up from sitting with some lack of ease, because their joints are stiffening, but they certainly aren't all dodderers, and though their voices may be rather more breathy and deliberate than those of young people, they don't necessarily become a tremolo-ridden treble.

Expertise

It is sometimes quite difficult for amateurs to portray convincingly a character who is called upon to show his expertise on stage—for example, you may be a doctor examining a patient, or perhaps you have to mime playing the piano (your hands, we hope, if you cannot play, invisible to the audience, but the upper part of your body and your head in clear view), or you might be a craftsman of some kind who has to show his skill during the play. Go to a doctor or a pianist or the appropriate craftsman, or to whatever sort of expert it may be, and ask to be shown how to do it. Don't be shy—most people like talking about their expertise and are flattered by such a consultation.

Heavy Loads

If you are supposed to be carrying something heavy, make it look as though you are actually doing so. If the load is a suitcase, it is probably worth filling it with something of the appropriate weight. For anything else which is in fact a light-weight prop but is meant to look heavy, try to lift the real thing or something of similar weight, if you can, and then reproduce the movements in rehearsal.

Slaps

It is very difficult to slap someone's face convincingly on the stage, and even more so to have your face slapped without flinching in anticipation. If you are the slappee, you just have to stay still, try to forget what is about to happen, and suffer if need be. If you are the slapper, you really do have to appear to put some venom into it and hit hard. You can avoid damaging the slappee too badly if you keep your hand loose and aim for the cheek rather than the jaw. Some people advocate hitting the side of the neck rather than the face, but in practice it seems more difficult to keep the aim true, and the slappee is quite likely to get a painful clout around the ear.

If you can avoid it, don't wear rings on the hand you slap with.

Fights

Fights need to be most carefully worked out and rehearsed if they are to look effective. Work out the moves in slow motion first and gradually speed them up. As with slaps, you have to look as though you mean it, and those involved should be prepared to find the experience painful, though of course no serious damage must be done. Obviously, punches must be pulled, and the effect of a blow can be softened anyway if the actor being struck moves very slightly away as it lands.

Don't forget the value of sound—grunts, squeals and pant-ing for breath can add greatly to the effect.

If you have to fight with swords or rapiers, it is highly likely that you will not have the weapons available until the dress rehearsal, but walking sticks can substitute at rehearsals. Try to avoid the sequence of sword blows that look too carefully planned—the up-down, up-down clashes. Meticulous rehearsal will allow one of the swordsmen to wield his blade fractionally after the other, so that he really seems to be parrying a thrust, the whereabouts of which he could not be certain of until it was made.

Any kind of blow which lands on the body, and this includes stabbing and kicking, is best contrived by placing the actors so that it is on the upstage side of the victim and the audience cannot see it actually reach its target. Gone, we hope, are the days when actors were run through with a sword carefully positioned between the arm and the side of the body and held there by the victim, but even that tired old cliché can be used if it is not clear to the spectators that that is what has happened.

Kicks are most frequently administered to a recumbent body, in which case the foot is driven on the stage rather than into the victim, whose jerking reactions and groans will supply verisimilitude. If you are called upon to attack another actor in this way, again you must rehearse carefully. Try it on your own with a cushion doing duty for the kickee's body, and teach yourself to control your foot with precision.

Shooting on stage can be done with a blank-firing gun, or by using a toy gun with an appropriate sound effect off stage. If you are shooting blanks, remember that a small wad may be ejected, which could hurt the victim if you are too close to him, so aim slightly upstage of him and, if possible, from some distance away. Never ever point the gun at the audience, even if it is not loaded, or shoot it towards them.

Falling

The first rule about falling on stage (or indeed if landing with a parachute) is to relax the body and limbs completely. Spectacular falls from a height or down a flight of stairs are matters for the expert, and probably best not attempted by amateurs, but if you have to faint or fall after being shot, drop first to your knees, then topple over on to one hip and finally let the torso go down, cushioning the fall with your arms. It will look quite effective, provided that you combine these movements into one swift and continuous action. Alternatively it may be appropriate to use furniture to break your fall.

If you have to fall forwards, keeping the body rigid, as Millington must in *Conduct Unbecoming*, you need to do it with courage, knowing that you can break the fall at the very last moment with your hands. Practise first with something soft to fall on. If you have to fall rigidly backwards, you will normally have to do so only if there is someone to catch you. Again, rehearse it well, and have faith in the catcher.

Dying

The biggest problem about dying on stage is not the moment of death, but what might legitimately be called the life hereafter. Corpses don't breathe, but living actors must, and their breathing when they are supposed to be dead is often visible to the audience. If possible, when you have fallen to the floor, have your back to the audience. If you can't do this, at least try to breath shallowly. Loose clothing may help to hide the movement of chest and abdomen.

Stage Blood

Stage blood can be purchased from theatrical suppliers. You can get it in capsule form—slip a capsule into your mouth, bite it at the appropriate moment, and you can produce a grisly flow from your lips. If you are to be shot or stabbed, put the blood in a small plastic bag with an open top (the bags that banks use for coins are very suitable), pin it under your shirt or dress, and at the moment of being wounded a smart upward blow to the region where the bag is concealed will make the blood spurt out and stain the clothing effectively. It is said to wash out easily, but even when diluted often leaves a pink stain, so it is as well to use it only with old clothes.

THE DRESS REHEARSAL

Before the dress rehearsal begins have a really good look at the stage. You need to be sure of exactly where the entrances and exits are (and they may not be quite as you have rehearsed), and of how doors open and shut, and of the position and size of the furniture (which may vary considerably from the make-do substitutes you have had up till now). Try to fix the various pieces of furniture in your mind in relation to one another, so that you know how far from the settee the easy chair is, and precisely where the bureau has been placed, and so on. This applies particularly if the scene is the home of the character you are playing. We know our own homes well—we can sit in a chair without groping for it or even looking to see where it is. Incidentally, if you have to sit, it is sometimes possible to position yourself without having to look round if your attention should be firmly fixed on something else, by feeling the edge of the chair with the backs of your legs.

Look for anything on the stage which may be awkward for you in some way—a rug or the sill at the bottom of a door over which you might trip, or the fact that the table on which you have to put that tray is smaller than you expected, or the gap between the settee and the bookcase which, now that the real furniture is there, is so narrow that you will barely be able to squeeze through it.

Particularly if you have not been able to rehearse on the stage or in a room large enough to simulate it, make sure of the time you will need for entrances and exits, and indeed for any moves. It may be necessary to start moving earlier than you have been accustomed to doing in rehearsal.

You must also be familiar with the backstage lay-out. You will need to know the position of the braces that support the scenery and of other obstacles, and you may have to find out how to get from one side of the stage to the other without being seen by the audience. Check where the props table is if you have to collect any properties. The more you know about the backstage area, the better, especially as it may be in darkness during the play.

If you have personal properties in the play, make a list of those that you require for each scene, so that you can check that you have them with you at the appropriate times. In the same way, if you have a number of costume changes, a list of exactly what you wear for each scene, not forgetting accessories like collar studs or earrings, can be very helpful.

Particularly if your costume changes are quick ones, arrange your clothes in the dressing-room so that each item is ready in the order in which you put it on. Establish a routine for yourself in such matters, which you will continue to follow during the performances.

When the rehearsal begins, try to convince yourself that it is not a rehearsal, but a performance, and put your heart and soul into it. Don't be discouraged or grumble if things go wrong or if there are long delays. And don't lose your temper. One of the prime purposes of dress rehearsals, especially the first, is to discover any problems and put them right.

Dress rehearsals often go on very late. Unless I know that something is going to be provided, I like to take a small snack with me. But that may be just a personal quirk.

7

The Set

Curtain Sets

A really well designed, constructed and painted set adds a tremendous amount to an amateur production. It can not only 'place' the play in either a specific location or period or both, but can also establish a mood for both audience and actors. Nevertheless, it is entirely possible to put on a show effectively without elaborate scenery, or indeed without any scenery at all, as is evidenced by many open-air productions and most of those in the round, when the setting is usually restricted to a few pieces of furniture or perhaps a tree stump or something of that sort.

On the other hand, if you are to perform on the proscenium stage, it may not be essential to have flats or to make what is known as a box set (that is, flats which go round the sides and back of the stage, totally enclosing the acting area), but you will almost certainly need to have curtains, which will give you an even-coloured background, hiding the walls of the stage and providing wing space at the sides to allow of entrances and exits. Against this background, furniture and perhaps cut-outs or groundrows (see page 114) can be added to give atmosphere and to suggest a scene. It is sometimes surprising to discover how willing audiences are to use their imagination, and they will accept a virtually unadorned curtain set as the hall of a stately home or another part of the forest or almost anything you choose.

The curtains, which are of course in addition to *the* curtain which divides the stage from the auditorium, need to be of the full height of the stage, arranged in the form of one or more sets of tormentors, or wing curtains, and drapes to cover the back and possibly the sides of the stage. The tormentors should preferably be about two metres wide, but could be no more than one metre if the stage is a small one. If suspended from bars, they can be turned so that in effect they form side curtains. The curtains at the back and sides are more useful if they are made up of a number of strips, which will allow flats to be inserted if you wish. You may also require borders or valences (narrow frills going across the stage immediately under the ceiling) to hide any lighting fixed above the stage area, and 'travellers' (curtains which can be drawn across the stage to alter its depth) add greater flexibility in the use you can make of the stage.

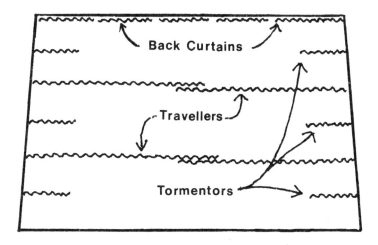

The best colour for stage curtains is a light grey or fawn. The more neutral the colour, the easier it will be to achieve different effects by varying the colour of the lighting, but white curtains will glare too much and show dirt too readily. Black can be extremely effective, but is not really suitable for comedies. Velvet or velour curtains are very desirable, but beyond the pockets of most amateur groups, and in fact almost any plain material will do. The curtains should be full enough to hang in folds when you want them to.

Ideally, you might aim at having several sets of curtains, but of course this involves not only expense, but the problem of storage.

Flats

Flats might be described as light-weight, portable sections of wall. They used always to consist of canvas or hessian stretched on a wooden frame and then painted, but nowadays many local fire authorities insist that fire-proof hardboard, nailed to the framework, should be used.

Flats for amateurs are usually built to the height of the stage ceiling, but if you have the good fortune to have a very high ceiling (perhaps even so lofty that you can 'fly' a change of set—that is, have parts of your setting suspended on ropes by means of which you can lower them to stage level or raise them above the acting area and out of the sight of the audience), you will probably not make them more than five or six metres high, beyond which they will be extremely difficult to manage. Some companies have flats which are much lower than the height of the stage and make up the difference by fixing narrow flats lengthways along the top of the main flats.

Flats come in all sorts of widths. Two metres is, again for ease of handling, about the practical maximum, but a number of different widths will allow you to alter the shape of the set and its size, and perhaps to make it more interesting by varying the angles.

If you are using flats which do not reach to the ceiling of the stage—perhaps when you perform in a professional theatre, using your own scenery—it is a good idea to darken the top of the flats, shading the top thirty centimetres or so from grey to black. Then, presuming that the lighting is focused on the acting area and the surroundings of the set are in darkness, the flats will merge into the darkness rather than forming a hard line against it.

Not all flats are plain. Door flats, for instance, are constructed so that they make a frame in which a door may be hung. It is necessary to provide a sill for rigidity, and this is best done with a flat strip of iron—a wooden sill is a tripping hazard for the actors. A window flat has an oblong or square cut out of it. Unless you are inserting a practical window frame into the opening, you can make it look more like a window by putting battens across the hole to divide it into panes, or stretch narrow black tape across the opening to give a lattice effect. Do remember to tell the actors not to put their hands through the non-existent glass.

Flats may be joined together by battens of wood, but although this gives good rigidity, it is time-consuming both when putting up and taking down the set, when all the battens have to be screwed on or taken off. More usually flats are secured together by means of ropes. Attach the rope to one flat by means of a hole bored through the upright on one side of the framework, near the top, or through an eye-screw in that position, and secure it to the neighbouring flat by a cleat fixed to the upright on the adjacent side of that flat, near to the bottom.

When you have joined two or more flats together, there will inevitably be visible cracks at the joins, and many societies paper over them. Of course, the paper has to be painted to match. Other groups, once they have erected their set, use wallpaper rather than painting the flats. Apart from the expense, this may not find favour with the fire authorities.

When you have constructed a box set, by joining the flats together, it may be rigid enough to stand up by itself, but any individual flats and probably the box set will need supports. Adjustable braces are best, and can be purchased . At one end is a double hook, one prong of which is passed through an eye-screw fixed to the frame of the flat. The length of the brace is then adjusted so that the bottom end of it reaches the floor at an angle which will give support. At the bottom end is a hinged piece of wood which lies flat on the floor, and it can be held in position there by placing a heavy weight such as a small block of concrete, or sandbags, over it. Alternatively you can construct a simple triangular frame of wood and attach it to the foot of the flat.

Braces can be screwed to the floor of the stage to secure them, but screwing anything into the stage is not usually a good idea for amateurs. The owners of the hall are unlikely to approve, and even if you own your own hall you should perhaps think twice before damaging it in this way.

Rostra

If I were starting an amateur company from scratch and had

some willing carpenters available, I would ask them to make me rostra before they started on flats. Rostra, in a large variety of sizes and heights, are extremely versatile. They can form platforms or steps or if tall enough can supply an extension to the front of the stage, and they can be used, suitably decorated, as furniture of a fairly primitive kind, while the opportunities they give for variety in grouping, or in simply adding the interest of different levels to a set, are invaluable. For ease of storage, a rostrum can be made with hinged sides which will fold flat, and a top that is lipped so that the underneath of it will fit snugly into the sides and hold them rigid.

A useful adjunct to your rostra is a short section of banisters. Form the rostra into steps, attach the banisters to one side, and place them so that they lead off stage, and you have the beginnings of a staircase to the imaginary floor above.

Backings

Doors, arches, windows and the like will probably require some kind of backing to suggest, however simply, that something other than the darkness of the backstage area lies beyond the set itself. Backings can be flats or a backcloth, painted simply or with quite elaborate scenes, according to what is appropriate.

Cut-outs and Groundrows

Cut-outs are usually made of hardboard which, as the name suggests, has been cut to represent perhaps a tree, or a pillar, or a fragment of wall, or a statue.

Groundrows in the scenery sense (the term is also used in lighting) are usually long narrow flats placed lengthways on the stage, with a cut-out attached to them, to represent a city skyline or a group of bushes or something similar. Such free-standing pieces can be supported by small struts, rather like a photo frame.

Cyclorama

A cyclorama is, technically, a curved white backing to the stage on which lighting can be used to give various effects, but in the amateur theatre the term is often applied to a white or neutral coloured backcloth (that is, a sheet of canvas attached at the top and the bottom to battens, and capable of being rolled up when not in use), or even to the plain back wall of the stage. If you are using the back wall in this way, you may need to disguise things like electric sockets.

Gauzes

The material for gauzes can be purchased from theatrical suppliers, or they can be hired. Lit from the front only, a gauze will hide what is behind it, and if you have painted a scene on it, it will look much like a backcloth. But if you now take down the front of house lighting and bring up the lighting on the stage behind the gauze, it and its painted scene will virtually disappear from view, though whatever is to be seen on stage behind the gauze will have a slightly hazy appearance. A gauze is often used in pantomime, or for a dream sequence.

Drugget

A drugget or floor cloth which can be spread over the stage helps to deaden the sound of the actors' footsteps. Most stages in halls used by amateurs are hollow, and something of the sort is needed if the actors, however lightly they tread, are not to sound like so many elephants. An old carpet is better than nothing, provided that it isn't so full of holes that the actors will trip in it, but if you have a balcony from which the audience will be able to see the floor of the stage, you will have to be sure that any floor covering you use is appropriate for your set. For this reason a neutral-colour canvas drugget which will cover the entire stage area is best, and if you want to be more decorative you can lay a carpet over it.

The Curtain

Make sure before the staging rehearsal that all curtains work smoothly. This is particularly important for the proscenium curtain, or front curtain. Most of the other curtains will be drawn when the front curtain is down or closed, so they can be adjusted if something goes wrong with them, but a front curtain that jerks or sticks is a disaster.

There has been a fashion in the last twenty years or so to dispense with the proscenium curtain altogether. The scene is set when the audience enters the auditorium, and indeed some of the actors may already be on the stage. Scene changes are often made in full view of the audience. The beginning of the play is signalled only by the dimming out of the house lights and the bringing up of the lights on stage to full brightness. It can be very effective, as it was in Roy Dotrice's marvellous one-man show based on Aubrey's *Brief Lives*. Of course it has to be done for a presentation in the round. But in general I feel that this idea should only be used when there is some real justification for it, because it always seems to me that the drawing or raising of the curtain to reveal to the audience a scene which they have not seen before is one of the moments of real magic in the theatre, and it's a pity to lose it.

Incidentally, unless it is essential that the actors should be speaking immediately on the curtain rise or during it, a very slight pause, during which the audience can take in the scene, is often very effective.

The Set Designer

Obviously, before you can begin to build a set you must know what you want it to look like. Some societies are lucky enough to have a set designer—lucky, that is, if he understands the function of a set, which is to serve the play and the actors, and not to be an end in itself. Some designers seem to feel that it is unfortunate that actors have to appear at all, and would prefer the play to take place by means of disembodied voices, while the audience gazes in rapture at the undefiled masterpiece which is their setting—and if you think I am exaggerating, believe me, I am not!

The set designer must also see eye to eye with the director about what is needed. He must read the play carefully and appreciate its demands, and of course he must know the stage well and understand what is possible on it and what is not.

If you are fortunate enough to have a large stage, the

designer should remember that some plays demand for some or all of their scenes a fairly intimate atmosphere, and if he is using a box set, he may consider bringing in the flats to make a smaller acting area. (The same applies if you are using a fixed curtain set, when you may wish to concentrate the acting area, the lighting, and perhaps the furniture in the centre of the stage, rather than using its entire width and depth, or to reduce the size of the stage with travellers, if you have them.)

The set designer's plans and drawings will include not only the shape of the set, the position of doors, windows, stairs and so on, but also an idea of where the furniture will be placed and what kind of furniture it will be. And of course he will select the colour of the set, bearing in mind that the background should not be too light, even for a comedy, for the actors' faces have a tendency to disappear if the scenery is too pale, nor too bright and hard a colour, nor too 'busy' a background, which may be very distracting and make it difficult for the audience to see what is going on in front of it. Any pattern should therefore be subdued.

Incidentally, a pattern can be applied to flats to give the appearance of wallpaper, by cutting a sponge and applying it, with the appropriate colour, to the background coat, once the latter has dried. Emulsion paints, with a matt finish, are best. Gloss paints will reflect the lights with an unpleasant effect.

It is extremely helpful if the set designer can produce a model of the set, because it makes it so much easier than a mere plan for the actors, and indeed the director, to visualize the final version.

The Stage Director

The stage director's job is to construct, paint and erect the sets for the play. He will read the play and discuss it with the set designer and the director, often giving practical advice, and he will also be aware of what furniture is required, some of which he and his team may have to make.

He will undoubtedly need a group of helpers, and it is preferable to have people who know something of carpentry and decorating. Some societies are forced to call on all their members to help with the set, but unskilled assistance is often more trouble than it is worth. Whether or not his team is made up of experts, the stage director must be firmly in control of them and be sure that they know exactly what they have to do.

According to the complexity of the set or sets he is making, he needs to have a detailed timetable, so that everything will be ready in time for the technical or staging rehearsal. Many amateurs experience from time to time the ghastly kind of dress rehearsal which is accompanied by constant hammering by the stage director and his staff, or even their presence, paint brushes in hand, on the set, while they finish it off. It isn't fair on anybody.

If you have an inexperienced team engaged in the construction of flats and other items for the stage, do warn them not to make everything too solid, and not to feel that all the joints and finishes have to be worthy of a master cabinet-maker. I remember one willing and highly skilled carpenter who built a set which was most beautifully put together and as strong as a house; unfortunately, it weighed a ton, and was almost impossible to move when we came to a scene change.

Because flats must be easily portable, they are necessarily somewhat flimsy, and especially if they are canvas-covered, you are liable to find that the whole set shakes when someone closes a door, and if they have to slam it, the action is rarely convincing, not only because the flats quiver, but because the door itself is too light. Nevertheless, I think this is preferable to giving your stage hands hernias by the use of solid and heavy flats. The only solutions are to make your door flats more firmly constructed than the rest, to ensure that the whole set is as rigidly fastened together as possible, and to instruct the actors that they must do their best to give the impression of slamming the door when in fact they close it fairly gently!

Scene Changes

The stage director's construction team will probably double as scene-shifters, and while the stage manager is in charge of performances and must see that everything is in its correct position before the curtain goes up on each scene, the stage director will be responsible for the way the scenery is physically changed and set.

It is vital to rehearse scene changes, and to make sure that all the stage hands know exactly what they have to do and in which order, especially when not only the flats have to be changed but bulky furniture has to be taken on and off the stage.

The stage director should work out all the changes in detail before the staging rehearsal, at which they can be practised. Not only is it essential to know the order in which each piece is set or struck (removed), but the stage hands must be told precisely where everything that they take off the stage is to be placed, and where everything that they will bring on is to be found. This is particularly important if your wing space is restricted. To ensure that the new setting is placed in its correct position, and this applies particularly to furniture, mark the stage with adhesive tape, using various colours as necessary.

It is only when the set changes have been meticulously planned and rehearsed, that scenes can be set without the long delays that are all too frequent in the amateur theatre. Usually the stage hands are too few in number and the space is too limited to make a lightning change, but good organization will cut down the delays. When possible, I would suggest that it is desirable that the stage director himself should not have to shift scenery and furniture—it is much better that he should supervise, especially since he may not have the same helpers every night and not all of them may be as well rehearsed as he would like. He can also keep stray actors out of the way.

Fireproofing

Most local authorities insist that everything on the stage which is part of the setting should be fireproofed. This applies not only to stage curtains and flats, but to the curtains which hang at the window in your set, even though you have lent them from your own home. Find out in advance what is required in your area, and prepare accordingly.

In some areas firemen come round to inspect the auditorium, to see that seats are battened in accordance with regulations, that exits are unobstructed and have independently lit exit signs (the illumination usually being supplied by night-lights rather than by electricity from the mains), and to check that the stage area is reasonably uncluttered, and that the materials of the set are non-inflammable. They will put a lighted match to curtains or flats, or to flowers or anything else on the stage that takes their fancy. Woe betide you if they succeed in making something burn, for quite apart from the damage, the official may insist on the cancellation of the show.

In order to fireproof flats and materials they should be soaked or liberally sprayed with a fireproofing solution which is available from theatrical suppliers. Or you can make it up for yourself, using 15 oz boric acid and 10 oz sodium phosphate to a gallon of water, or for delicate fabrics, 8 oz boric acid and 10 oz borax to a gallon of water. Wherever possible use materials which are already fireproofed when you buy them.

Furniture

Hiring furniture is a very expensive business, especially if you need period pieces, on which the insurance is high. Sometimes hiring is inescapable if you want the play to look right— Victorian furniture may be old, but it isn't old enough if you are putting on a Restoration play. For more recent plays it is very often possible to borrow furniture from members of the society, but if they offer to lend something, whoever is in charge of furniture should make sure that it is really suitable— the three-piece suite that someone has kindly said you can have may be so bulky that it will completely fill the stage, or the little table so aggressively modern that it just doesn't fit for *Pink String and Sealing Wax*.

If you have storage space available, it may be worth collecting various items of furniture, especially if they are Victorian or earlier, which often allows them to be used in contemporary as well as period plays.

Furniture can often be made to look more suitable for your play by covering it with material, or by painting it.

8

Lighting

General Principles

Lighting for the stage is a great mystery for many amateurs. The very first thing to be said about it is that, though good and imaginative lighting can add immensely to the effectiveness of a production, a play can be performed without any lighting at all, and I do not mean only in the open air. The daylight that comes into a hall which is well provided with windows, provided that a reasonable amount of it reaches the stage, can prove adequate. After dark it is quite possible to put on a play using only the ordinary lighting available in the hall, even if it means that the audience is fully lit too.

However, the magic of the theatre is always increased, I believe, when the auditorium lights go out and the curtains open to reveal a well-lit stage. Moreover, stage lighting concentrates the audience's attention on the stage, separates the actors and their surroundings and story from the world outside, and gives the actors a greater sense of being performers. Like scenery, lighting can establish place and period, or help to do so, and can be of major importance in setting the mood of the scene.

A well-lit scene, incidentally, is not necessarily brightly lit—I was referring to the quality of the lighting rather than its power. Obviously, you do not have all the lamps on full for a night scene, or one set in a dark forest. However, it is absolutely vital to remember that the audience wants to see the scenery and particularly the actors (above all, their faces), and never in a quest for realism should you allow the scene to be so under-lit, at least for more than a very short time, that they cannot do so. A compromise must always be reached between lighting that provides the right atmosphere and the need for clear visibility, with the latter being of greater importance.

If you insist on very dim, atmospheric lighting, you may be able to achieve the desired effect by beginning with your under-lit stage, and slowly bringing in more light as the scene progresses, so that there is sufficient illumination for the actors to be seen. Even so, this technique cannot be used satisfactorily if the early lines of the scene are of major significance, and in any case the lighting will have to be brought up so gradually that the audience is barely aware of the change while it is happening.

In the same way, though it is sometimes very effective to have lighting only behind the actors, producing a silhouette effect, you will need a faint glimmer on the actors' faces, and generally speaking this device can work only for a short period and preferably when the action that the audience sees is exclusively or mainly in dumb-show.

Now, in order to light the actors adequately, the position of the lanterns is a prime consideration. Some halls where amateurs perform have stage lights only behind the proscenium arch, and this means that they tend to be directed downwards, illuminating the tops of the actors' heads and leaving their faces heavily shadowed. In this case, it is virtually essential to have those old-fashioned contraptions, footlights, which will throw light upwards and counteract the effect of the overhead lighting. In passing, it is worth mentioning that to achieve a natural effect, since in real life only reflected light reaches us from the floor, the footlights should never be as bright as those overhead. Floodlights beamed across the stage from the wings may be an alternative to footlights, and cross lighting of this kind can be very interesting, but the light from floods is not easy to control, and they often have to be placed in positions which obstruct entrances and exits.

Lighting from the auditorium is much more satisfactory, if it has to be on its own, than lighting behind the proscenium arch, and provided that the lanterns do not shine down on the stage at too steep an angle, will obviate the need for footlights. On the other hand, the beams from front of house lighting should not travel to the stage at too flat an angle, for this has the effect of partially eliminating the contours of the actors' faces.

Ideally, you need a large number of lanterns—some fixed in the hall, others immediately behind the proscenium arch, and a third set above the stage halfway towards the back. Lighting behind the proscenium arch is almost essential in order to eliminate unpleasant shadows from the front of house lamps; you will never cut them out altogether, however, and it is a mistake to think that you can do so by adding more and more lanterns, but you can soften their sharpness and darkness by judicious positioning of spots and floods.

In addition, you may need such items as a follow spot (a spotlight which can be moved to follow an actor as he moves about the stage, or to use outside the normal acting area without having to use one of your other lanterns for this purpose), floods (large lanterns which give a general light and are often used to illuminate areas beyond the set, such as the scene outside a window, or so that when a character exits through a door he does not do so into pitch darkness), ground-rows (a row of lights at floor level used mainly to illuminate a cyclorama), special lighting effects for various kinds of weather—lightning or snow or moving clouds, for instance—or for fires, not to mention strobes, ultra-violet lamps and the like.

Many different styles and effects may be needed in one scene, and a full-length play may have hundreds of lighting cues, so it is obvious that the more lanterns you have, the more easily you will be able to change the lighting, using one set at one time and others at other times.

If you are putting on a one-set play, with all scenes taking place at the same time of day and therefore without any change in lighting, you have far fewer problems. But beware of using every single lantern that you have in a case like this, even if the play is a comedy, for which lighting should usually be quite bright. As with everything else in the theatre, variety is very desirable, and even a brightly lit stage needs to have some areas which are more strongly lit than others. Arrange these pools of light so that they cover those parts of the acting area where the most important action takes place, or where the principal characters are likely to spend much of the time. Remember too that in real life rooms are not evenly lit. There is more light by a window, or in the immediate vicinity of the room's lamps.

Try to cover the various areas of the stage with at least two lanterns for each, reaching it at different angles. Lanterns should rarely be trained down to their own side of the stage—angle those on the right so that they illuminate the centre or left of the stage, and vice versa, and those in the centre to left or right.

You may wish to illuminate brightly a single small area of the stage, and in that case the shorter the distance the beam has to travel, the sharper the lit area will be. All lights have a certain amount of spill (mostly reflected light) which will make it difficult to limit the area too closely, especially on a small stage. Most lanterns can be focused down to provide a thin beam, which may give the desired effect, and indeed the focusing of all the lamps you use is an important factor in getting suitable lighting with plenty of variety.

The cyclorama is often used to represent the sky, and all kinds of interesting effects can be achieved by the colours of the lighting you use on it. If you light it solely with a ground-row, the colour will fade towards the top of the cyclorama, and it is better to have overhead lighting as well, if you can, so that the light is evenly distributed over it.

Spotlights and Dimmers

There are two main kinds of spotlights—the profile spot, which gives a hard-edged beam, and the fresnel spot,which, having a more complex lens, gives a softer-edged light. In general, only the profile spot is used from front of house positions. The wattage of spotlights can vary from 250w to 5,000w, but for most halls and small theatres, 1,000w will be adequate. The bulbs do burn out now and then, and it is a good idea to have some spares, though they are rather expensive.

Lanterns of all the types you will need can be hired, but if you make a profit on your productions you should consider purchasing your own. The same applies to that vital piece of equipment the dimmer board. Dimmers enable you to vary the intensity of the lights connected to them, from nothing to a very faint gleam and gradually up to full brightness. Dimmers used to come as separate units, but are more often found nowadays on a board containing a number of dimmer channels.

The dimmer is an enormous help in getting variety into your lighting, quite apart from the ability it gives you to bring the lights up slowly on a scene, or gradually to darken the stage (still remembering to have enough light for the audience to see). You can of course experiment with various intensities of light at the staging rehearsal, recording the position of the controls on the dimmers when the desired effect has been obtained, so that in performance it can be repeated without having to seek for it in a hit or miss way.

It is highly desirable that your house lights should be attached to a dimmer. When your play is about to begin, you take the house lights down slowly, which not only gives the audience a sense of anticipation and time to finish off their conversations, but also avoids plunging them into sudden darkness and then, while their eyes are still adjusting to that, equally suddenly presenting them with a brightly lit stage.

Blackouts

If you want to have a perfect blackout, perhaps at the end of a scene, it is essential to have a master switch which will control all the stage lighting, so that it can all be extinguished with one simple movement. After the blackout you will almost certainly have to bring the lights up again gradually to avoid blowing a fuse. During the blackout, therefore, you must bring all the dimmer controls to zero, and when you switch the master control on again, bring the lights up quickly but steadily.

Jellies

The lighting from any kind of lantern is usually coloured by means of 'jellies'—gelatine slides which are slipped over the lenses of the lamps and which come in a large variety of colours. A combination of colours is most effective—golds and pinks for a warm effect, blues and greens for colder lighting. If, as has been suggested, you are using two lanterns to illuminate the same area of the stage, it is a good idea to use jellies of different colours—for instance, straw or gold in one, and salmon or pink in the other.

When selecting the jellies to give the atmosphere you want, it is worth remembering that they will have an effect on the scenery, the costumes and the make-up. Check at the staging rehearsal or the first dress rehearsal to see that your carefully produced atmosphere does not result, for example, in all the reds on the stage turning brown or even black.

Why use jellies at all? Quite simply because without them the lighting will appear very harsh and clinical, and will lack any sense of mood.

Special Effects

Lighting can be used to produce all kinds of special effects. You can get strobe equipment, for example, or with a projector you can produce a snow effect, or make clouds move across the sky on your cyclorama. You can also shape the light or project shadows of various kinds by cutting a mask to fit over the lens. You could project a transparency to make a background picture. The great problem is to position the projector so that it does not illuminate the actors and so that the image is not distorted because it has to be projected from the side rather than from straight in front. In a professional theatre it is sometimes possible to project from behind the screen, but there is rarely room for this in the halls used by amateurs.

Firelight

A lighted fire is often simulated by an ordinary light bulb, placed in the grate of your fireplace, and covered with crumpled pieces of gelatine. You need to have some kind of frame over the bulb so that the strips of jelly do not touch it, which would probably make them melt or burn. Firelight, even from embers, is much more orange than red, so make sure that the jellies you use include ambers and golds. Warn the actors not to poke the fire so vigorously that they shatter the light bulb!

The Source of Light

An interior scene on the stage is normally lit much more brightly than it would be in real life. We have all seen those plays in which a single candle apparently provides thousands of watts of illumination. Audiences generally accept this distortion of reality quite happily, but I think they like to have some sense of where the light comes from. In daylight, there is usually a window, and if there is a strong light outside it, possibly even beamed into the room, that will suffice. If it is dark outside, include lamps, if you can, as appropriate to the scene.

Such lamps should not be practical as far as the actors are concerned—they should not be able to turn them on or off by means of switches on the stage, though they may pretend to do so. Instead, they should be controlled by the lighting staff, so that when turned on, the stage lighting can be increased in a synchronized fashion with them. If this is not done, you will often have the actor on stage switching on the light, and the general lighting coming up a few seconds later—or even the other way round, which is worse. The actor pretending to switch on a lamp must keep his hand on the switch until the light, controlled by the lighting staff, comes on.

The Lighting Director

As with all other members of the backstage staff, the lighting director must have a full understanding of the play and the director's intentions, and will make his lighting plan in accordance. Of course, he must know what he is doing with electricity and be fully aware of the capabilities of the equipment available.

If any lighting changes take place during scenes, he must be in a position from which he can see the stage, and for this reason it may be worth taking the trouble to wire his controls to the back of the hall.

The lighting director is responsible for the rigging of the lighting—that is, hanging the lanterns and training them at the required angles on to the stage. Stands to support lanterns may be bought or hired, and are usually used for floods, which, even if angled, produce a general light and do not have to be directed from a height. For spotlights, bars or some other form of mounting at a good height will be needed, and if these are not already a fixture in the hall you use, you might ask permission to set whatever you need in position and to leave it there permanently. This will simplify the job of hanging the lanterns before the show and taking them down afterwards.

It is absolutely vital that the lighting director should be aware of the maximum load that can be used on the electrical circuit in the hall where you perform. Many local halls are not equipped to cope with the wattage of even a modest number of lanterns all operating at full power at the same time (especially if other electrical appliances are also in use—heaters, ovens, tea-urns, and the like), and if you overload, the main fuses will blow. This is another reason, by the way, why you should have dimmers, so that after a blackout you can bring the lights up gradually to full; to switch everything on simultaneously at maximum brightness may demand a surge of power which the system cannot provide, and another total and unwanted blackout may result. If you are in doubt about the hall's capacity in this respect, ask a professional electrician to advise you.

The Actor

Always take note at the dress rehearsal of what lighting you are given, where it comes from and where it falls on the stage. You may need to make minor adjustments to your positions on stage to ensure that you use the lighting to best advantage. This is particularly important if you are supposed at any point to be standing in a spotlight on an otherwise darkened stage. If it is a follow spot, whoever is operating it should pick you up, but if the person working it is a bit dozy or if it is a fixed spot, it is your responsibility to make sure that the light is on your face and that you don't move out of it.

9

Sound

The Sound Director

The person in charge of sound will of course have to read the play carefully, marking all the places where sound effects are required, and then set about obtaining recordings, or making them or preparing the equipment with which to produce them.

Very many effects can be put on tape, but there are several problems connected with the use of tape recorders. Firstly, there is the difficulty of getting the sound to come exactly when you want it to; separate your various recordings with leader tape and work out to the second when and where to start the tape so that the effect is heard at precisely the right moment. Secondly, you may have difficulty in making the sound come from the appropriate direction; this can be overcome by connecting the tape recorder to a number of loud speakers, placed in different positions, but of course you have to be careful to switch to the right one. Thirdly, the hum of the tape recorder and the click when it is switched on and off may be audible to the audience. None of these difficulties is insurmountable, and certainly the tape recorder is the best thing to use for car or aeroplane noises, or if you need the sound of a crowd or perhaps an explosion.

Making your own effects recording can be fun. Comparatively few actors—few in numbers, that is—can sound like a large crowd, especially if they make their noises fairly quietly. For the explosion of cans of rotten tomatoes at the end of Act One of *The Matchmaker*, I once had a tape recorder going while my wife and my two small children burst paper bags, dropped weights from the kitchen scales into metal buckets, knocked over a pile of food tins, broke glass into another bucket and crumpled a matchbox right next to the microphone. Barking was not meant to be included, and we had to shut the dog away for the second take. The final result, amplified, was very satisfactory.

Make sure that any sound effects during the play, especially if they are to continue for a long time, are not so loud that they drown the actors' voices. If, for instance, you need the effect of continuous rain, start it quite loudly, but after a very short time gradually reduce the volume so that it can still be heard, but is not obtrusive. Skilled use of the volume control is essential in many other cases, such as the approach of a car, or its departure.

Knocks and Rings

Many effects are better done on the spot by the sound director or possibly the stage manager, or in some cases by members of the cast. Knocking at a door, for instance, is often performed by the actor who is about to enter. A genuine door-knocker can be fixed to the wooden frame of the door flat, though some groups prefer to have it on a separate and permanent board, on which can also be screwed battery-operated door bells or chimes.

If a telephone has to ring you can use your door bell for it, but whoever is operating it must listen carefully to a real telephone—most people trying to reproduce the sound make the double rings follow each other too quickly. You should have sight of the stage so that you can see when the actor picks up the phone and the ringing stops. Ask the actor to pick it up between rings. If the play is set in America, or indeed almost anywhere other than Britain, you should not use the double ring, and many foreign phones have a lighter, more warbling tone than ours. If you keep a tape recorder running during an American film on television you will probably be able to pick up the authentic sound.

Slamming Doors

If a door has to be slammed off stage, and there is a suitable door in the backstage area which is also in the right direction, the best thing is to slam that. If not, you can get the effect by using a plank of wood. Lay it on the ground, put your foot on one end and raise the other end slightly by means of a piece of rope attached to it; release the rope sharply, and the resultant thud will sound reasonably like a door slamming.

Shattering Glass

Drop broken glass into a metal bucket.

Gunfire

Rifle fire or a shot from a revolver can be simulated by hitting the leather seat of a chair with a cane. Heavier guns require thumps on a bass drum.

Rain, Wind, Thunder and Lightning

The old-fashioned 'rain-box' is still the best bet for rain. Partly fill a wooden or cardboard box with dried peas—a little rehearsal in tipping it from one side to the other continuously will give you the effect of rain, and the speed and angle of the tipping can produce anything from a gentle shower to a downpour.

Thunder is usually produced with a thunder sheet, which is a sheet of metal, thin enough to be very slightly flexible, suspended by a rope so that nothing is touching it. Shake it, and you can produce the sound of thunder. The lightning is of course supplied by the lighting department flashing suitably positioned floods or spots on and off.

Wind can be simulated on a wind machine, which is a slatted wooden cylinder supported in a cradle and with a handle fixed to one end so that it can be turned; over it hangs a sheet of tough canvas. Turn the handle, holding the canvas down over the revolving slats, and depending on the speed with which you wind it, it will sound like a gentle zephyr or a howling gale.

All these weather effects are often provided nowadays from tape recordings.

Music

Music may be used during a play not only when one of the

actors is playing, or pretending to play, an instrument on stage, but also as a background. In a production of *Tobias and the Angel* I used electronic music, at a very low volume, whenever the Archangel Raphael was on stage. The character speaks in a very natural manner and there is comparatively little suggestion of his supernatural quality in his words; I felt that the music added just a hint of other-worldliness.

In a production of *A Midsummer Night's Dream* I used music to introduce each scene—fifteenth-century court music for Theseus and his court, part of *Façade* for the mechanicals, Delius' *Sleigh Ride* for the lovers, and electronic music for the immortals—but in this case it did not continue but was simply used to introduce the various scenes.

Music is frequently used before the curtain rises on each act and scene, and if you choose carefully, preferably avoiding anything too well known and certainly those pieces of music which have a familiar story attached to them, it can help considerably to set the mood. You have to judge the amount of music that you are going to use with some precision. The house lights go down, and as they do the music starts; if it goes on too long, the audience will be bored and may start to talk; if it stops too quickly, they will hardly have settled themselves.

Make sure that your stage manager knows at exactly which point in the music you want the curtain to rise or open, and don't let the sound director fade it out too quickly, especially if you are going to have a slight pause at the beginning to let the audience take in the scene. The music should be faded down slowly rather than cut off abruptly, and even if the play starts with the actors already talking, the sound can continue very softly for a few moments.

Opening and closing music is best put on to the tape recorder and amplified through speakers in the auditorium. Check the volume in advance—you don't want to blast the audience out of their seats, nor to have it so quiet that they are unaware of it.

The sound director may also be responsible for music that is to be played while the audience is coming in, during the intervals, and as the audience leaves. Personally, I think there is too much muzak around and prefer not to have such an accompaniment to my theatre-going. However, if you do use such music, try to make it reasonably suitable to the play that you are presenting. Pop music in the intervals of *The Country Wife* doesn't really sound right, any more than Mozart is the best background accompaniment if you're putting on *Zigger Zagger*.

10

Costumes

The Wardrobe Mistress

A good wardrobe mistress is a boon to any amateur group. She almost certainly needs to be a capable dressmaker (and have access to friends who are good with their needles), and she should have some knowledge of period costumes and a sense of style in dress. If the group has accumulated a wardrobe, she should be fully conversant with what is in it, and if she also has some idea of what other local societies have in their wardrobes, which she might be able to borrow, then she is indeed a pearl. The job is a major responsibility for one person, and she would be well advised to find someone to share it with her.

She may herself be able to design costumes, and if not, to work to someone else's drawings. She will know the value of accessories in transforming a simple costume into something more interesting and characteristic. She will also know that actors need to feel happy in their clothes, and that they should fit reasonably well. And she will never put an actor in a costume which is unsuitable for his character simply because it is available and happens to fit him. Good costumes help actors enormously. It is sometimes difficult for an amateur to feel that he or she is playing Richard II or Lady Teazle when rehearsing in sweater and jeans, but put him into kingly robes or her into the elaborate eighteenth-century dress, and the performance will suddenly take on a new reality.

Some wardrobe mistresses keep a card index of all members of the group with their vital statistics, which can save a lot of time in measuring. Unfortunately, waists and other parts of the anatomy don't always stay the same size, so unless she is really certain that no changes have taken place since the original measurements were taken, she will probably have to do the job again anyway.

Hiring

Of course, the easiest way of costuming a period play is to hire the lot. Apply to one of the costumiers who advertise in *Amateur Stage*, giving them as much notice as possible. They will send you measurement forms to fill in and return, and in due course the costumes will arrive—usually quite clean, if a little shabby. So will a pretty hefty bill. The costumiers do not exploit the amateurs—on the contrary—but their costs are high.

Unless the play is new or very little known, you will not need to tell them about the characters. They know the plays and what is suitable for each character, though if you want Hamlet to wear sky-blue instead of the usual black, you will have to make that clear. On the other hand, be sure that your instructions and measurements are clear, and be particularly meticulous over accessories, hats and shoes, which you may or may not want and which the costumiers may or may not supply automatically.

The costumes are usually sent out in a large hamper or skip. If you have them sent to the hall where you perform, you will need to make sure that someone will be there to receive them. Equally, of course, you will have to arrange for their return, in good order, after the show.

As suggested above, it is sometimes possible to borrow some or all of the costumes you need from another amateur group, and even if they charge a hire fee, it is likely to be a fraction only of what you will pay to a professional costumier. But very little choice will be available, and you will be lucky if you find suitable costumes that will fit.

Making Your Own Costumes

It is cheaper, though much more time-consuming, to make your own costumes, and provided that you have somewhere to store them, it is possible over the years to build up an extensive and useful wardrobe. You may be able to add to your group's income by hiring costumes to other amateurs, or at least bring in enough cash to pay for any necessary cleaning.

All kinds of materials are suitable for stage costumes, and members of a dramatic society should be encouraged to bring old curtains and their cast-off clothes to swell the group's wardrobe and stock of material. Jumble sales are a useful source of clothes which can be adapted, or sometimes worn as they are. It is also worth making an appeal in your local community for really old clothes; a surprising number of houses can turn out garments dating back to the 1920s and beyond, and you might find a frock coat or two, or top hats, or other such items which are of particular value because of the difficulty always experienced with men's clothes.

If you are making costumes for a play, of course you have to try to get the period right. There are many excellent books available which will give you pictures of the costumes worn in different ages, and tell you the kinds of materials and colours which were used. You do not have to be totally accurate, since few in your audiences will be costume experts, and even those are unlikely to jib if you have wandered a few years out of period. On the other hand, people do have a certain broad familiarity with costumes of past ages, which they have gained from paintings and the theatre, films and television, and they will know if things don't really look right. A group I know made themselves a magnificent wardrobe of eighteenth-century men's costumes, but unfortunately their designer was under the impression that the coat sleeves finished just below the elbow, so they all show almost a whole forearm of shirt sleeves, beautifully ruffled, but nevertheless spoiling the overall effect.

Don't forget what you can achieve with trimmings. Old pieces of lace, scarves, butter muslin, almost any other material, belts, costume jewellery, decorative buttons, braids, plaited string—there is no end to the things you can use to turn a basic costume into something which will look quite stunning. You do not have to spend hours in elaborate embroidery, or even in perfect stitching. Decoration on clothes can be painted on, braids and costume jewellery tacked on quite roughly. Incidentally, a skirt can be made to look fuller by painting dark streaks downwards on it to give the effect of folds in the material. All sewing need only be strong enough to survive the performances. It should go without saying that wherever possible you should avoid cutting the material, especially of existing costumes—tucks and hems will allow them to be let out or lengthened for future use.

Be careful about the colour of the costumes, bearing in mind the character for whom the costume is intended (obviously you don't dress the heroine of a melodrama in scarlet, and for that matter there are good reasons for Hamlet's traditional black), the colours of the setting, and the provision of a pleasing contrast and variety.

Many amateur groups feel that a wardrobe mistress is needed only for period plays or for costumes which cannot be described as everyday. But she should be involved in every production. If the actors are to wear their own clothes, she should make sure, in consultation with the director and the designer, that they are indeed suitable for the characters and that there is variety and that the colours are neither going to fade into the background of the set nor clash with it unpleasantly.

In The Round

If your performance is to be given in the round, the wardrobe mistress's job is likely to be more exacting, because the costumes will come under much closer scrutiny from the audience and any faking will be more apparent. Do not despair, for even in-the-round audiences will be to some extent indulgent, and a good overall effect will allow minor details to pass without too much notice.

Wearing Period Clothes

While many actors find that their costumes help their characterizations, others need to be taught how to wear period clothes. It may be the director's job to tell them how to walk and stand and sit, but the wardrobe mistress can help by explaining what was worn in the period concerned underneath the visible clothes. Corseting, for instance, which has been used in certain eras by men as well as women, has a major effect on posture.

Even in the early days of rehearsal for a period play, it is a good idea to get the actors to wear some kind of clothing which will help to give them the feel of their eventual costumes—long skirts for the ladies (really long ones, so that they are aware of them) and shoes with the right height of heel, and perhaps a raincoat for the men (so that they remember when they sit, for example, that they will have to deal with the coat tails of their costume). You might even consider, if you can obtain suitable corsets, putting the actors into them.

Some Costume Problems

Period costumes for men. After the Middle Ages, costumes for men are very difficult to make satisfactorily, unless you are prepared to go to considerable trouble and expense. Even so, a certain amount of ingenuity can work wonders. A naval overcoat worn in World War Two, plus a pair of sailor's bell-bottoms was cobbled into a very presentable topcoat for a highwayman. The bellbottoms were turned into a double cape attached to the overcoat, additional buttons were added so that they were grouped in pairs and all buttons were painted silver.

Victorian and Edwardian jackets and trousers can sometimes be approximately contrived out of a man's single-breasted contemporary suit by turning the lapels so that they are much smaller and higher (making an additional buttonhole if necessary) and by narrowing the trouser legs. A waistcoat will be needed, if only to hide the modern waistband of the trousers, but this need not necessarily be of the same material.

Chain mail. One of the standard jokes about amateurs is that they are addicted to knitted 'chain mail'. In fact, thick string or wool, loosely knitted and painted with aluminium paint, can look very effective, though it is difficult to fake the weight and discomfort that the real thing must have had. The trouble is, however, that there seems to be an Imitation Chain Mail Law which states that it has always been used before, with the result that it never fits, most of the paint has worn off, and it is often full of holes. It has also invariably been worn previously by someone who was too big for it, so that it bulges and droops in a most unrealistic way. If you make your own chain mail, ask the actors to treat it with great care, be prepared to make running repairs, preserve it carefully between plays, and make new sets if it doesn't fit properly.

Zips. Beware of using zip fasteners in period costumes. Unfortunately, they always look like zips. Besides, nervous actors specialize in making them jam. Velcro is probably the most useful kind of fastening, or failing that, old-fashioned hooks and eyes, even if they often mean that the actor can't do up a costume by himself and needs help.

Padding. If you have to make an actor look fat and really want to do the job well, the best thing is to hire padding from a theatrical costumier. As an alternative you can swathe the actor in towels or other thick material. The padding you can hire is hot, and towels are even worse. For a pot belly you may be able to arrange a cushion suitably beneath the actor's clothing, but it is often difficult to get the shape right, and you will have to secure it carefully, preferably with some kind of harness, so that it doesn't slip. The costume itself should, if possible, have a high collar and long sleeves, to hide the tell-tale neck and wrists of a thin actor, and should be tight over the padding of the torso, while the sleeves and trouser legs need to be baggy.

Bulky costumes. Doors and arches in sets are sometimes quite narrow, and if the play demands wide costumes, such as crinolines, the wardrobe mistress needs to be sure that the actors wearing them will be able to get on and off the stage without difficulty. I once played a Roman centurion in a Nativity play in a splendid hired costume which included metal shoulder pieces; unfortunately, these made my shoulders so broad that my entrance and exit through a narrow archway had to be made sideways, which did not exactly enhance the authority of the part.

Hats. It is often possible to concoct period hats out of ladies' wide-brimmed contemporary hats, especially with the addition of trimmings of various kinds. Since hats are worn far

less often than in the past, hang on to any you can
find. Wherever possible hats should be worn fairly well back
on the head rather than tilted forwards, since in the latter case,
with mainly overhead lighting, the actors' faces may be
shadowed.

Footwear.   Shoes and boots often present a great problem in
period plays, especially for men, and I sometimes think that it
is a good thing that in most amateur productions in halls where
the auditorium is not raked very few of the audience can see the
actors' feet. However, modern shoe styles are often more
adaptable than those of, say, twenty or thirty years ago when
laces were the rule. A man's black, slipper-style shoes can be
made to look reasonably in period if you cut a buckle out of
cardboard, paint it silver and thread it on to a circle of flat
black elastic which can be slipped over the shoe.

Riding boots can, in an emergency, be made by painting
rubber or plastic wellingtons in an appropriate colour and
adding a cuff of leather, either imitation or real. I'm afraid they
will still look like doctored wellingtons, but they may be better
than nothing.

Tights and stockings.   Men often have great difficulty in
keeping up tights or stockings so that they don't wrinkle, and
wrinkled stockings look awful, especially in plays set in a
period when men were meticulous about their appearance. An
old-fashioned suspender belt, of the kind that every lady used
to have in the days before tights became universal, is probably
the best answer. It may cause ribaldry in the gentlemen's
dressing-room, but the audience won't see it. If all else fails, a
coin twisted in the top of the stocking will act as a kind of
substitute garter. Tights can be kept taut by securing them to
braces.

The Dress Rehearsal

The director will undoubtedly want to check all the costumes
at the dress rehearsal, and the wardrobe mistress should do so
too. Don't forget to look for wrist-watches, which amateur
actors are often curiously reluctant to abandon. Wedding rings

may have to be removed or covered with flesh-coloured adhesive tape.

Of course it is usually too late to make major changes in the costumes and in any case the actors should have had an earlier opportunity to try them on and to discover any problems. However, the main function of a dress rehearsal is the discovery of last-minute snags, and the wardrobe mistress should come to it armed with all she may need to make alterations and adaptations.

Quick Changes

Some members of the cast may need to make very quick costume changes. If you are performing in a well-appointed theatre there may be a dressing-room close to the stage which can be used, but it is more likely that the amateur actor will have to change in the wings or just outside the stage area, possibly in semi-darkness and a very restricted space. If it is an extensive change, he will almost certainly need help. The wardrobe mistress should arrange for a dresser to be available. Try to have the same person (or possibly persons—though if there are more than two they will probably get in each other's way) each night, and make sure that they have the new costume carefully arranged in the order in which the actor will put the garments on and that they know exactly what he wants them to do. In other words, this must be carefully rehearsed.

Running Repairs

The wardrobe mistress should be on hand at all performances, ready to make running repairs to costumes. Sometimes actors have to be sewn into what they are wearing and unpicked at the end of the show. A good supply of safety pins can solve many problems.

It is useful too to have available some cleaning spirit with which to remove make-up marks, which are particularly troublesome on collars and other neckwear. I have known actors cover up such stains with white make-up, but a better answer is a quick dab of cleaner.

11

Make-up

In the days when I began working in the amateur theatre, it was the fashion for all of us to cover our faces with a thick layer of Nos. 5 and 9, to plaster our eyelids with dark blue for the men and light blue for the ladies, for the men to colour their lips heavily with one of the darker shades of carmine, and for all cheeks to be well rouged. Then, if it were a character part, one would cover all remaining areas of the face with a network of thick lines of lake, or even black, to represent wrinkles. Nowadays far less make-up is used, in the professional theatre too, and most amateurs have realized that a more natural effect is to be preferred.

Why use make-up at all, unless you want to change your appearance radically? Because stage lighting, even if it is not very powerful, has two effects on the actor's face—it makes him look pale, and it has a tendency to flatten the features; make-up can correct both problems. For most amateur productions, a straight character will, however, need a minimum of lightly applied make-up, and if you have good natural colour in your face or something of a tan, and if additionally the contours of your features are well marked, you may decide that a foundation will not be needed.

Basic Straight Make-up

The first question if you are going to put make-up on your face is whether or not you need to grease it first. It is certainly easier to apply and to remove make-up if you put on a base of removing or so-called vanishing cream, though if you have a greasy skin (and provided you have not just washed your face) you might manage without it. In any case, use the lightest of films—indeed, many actors put on a thin layer of cream and then gently wipe most of it off with a tissue, leaving only a trace behind.

If you are going to use a foundation make-up, it should again, unless the lighting is very strong, not be too heavy. There are many forms of make-up available—pancakes and liquid or semi-liquid make-ups in tubes—but many actors prefer the good old greasepaint in sticks, and swear by a mixture of No. 5 (a deep cream colour) and No. 9 (a kind of reddish brown) for their foundation. Apart from anything else, they will tell you, nothing is so redolent of the theatre as the unforgettable smell of greasepaint. Two schools of thought exist concerning the method of applying the make-up to your face: one suggests that you should paint fairly heavy streaks of make-up on your face and then carefully smooth it so that the colour is even all over; the other prefers to mix the greasepaint first on the palm of one hand and transfer it to the face with the fingers of the other hand. It really doesn't matter which procedure you follow as long as the colour is evenly spread, and that you don't forget to bring it well down the neck and on and around the ears, so as not to produce a mask-like effect.

If you apply a foundation of this kind, you will hide the natural colours of your face and therefore increase the flattening effect of the lights, so you now have to restore the contours of the face by adding shadows and highlights. A light-coloured make-up such as No. 5, or No. 20 (white) will be used for highlights, and the darker colours like No. 25 (lake) and No. 32 (dark grey) will give shadows. Most make-up seems to be better when you mix the basic colours together, and you can do the blending on your palm.

Exactly where you put the highlights and shadows depends on the effect you want to achieve. You may simply restore the bumps and hollows of your own face, or you may wish to change your appearance in some way—perhaps you want to make your cheeks plumper or thinner. It is surprising how easily the whole appearance can be altered in this way. It needs care and a certain amount of skill, but it always seems to me a pity that so few amateurs actors are capable of making themselves up. Make-up demonstrations are often arranged by groups or by drama associations and a great deal can be learned from them, but if they are not available to you, or even if they are, it is worth getting a make-up kit and a book on the subject. The book should perhaps come first, for it will almost certainly suggest what sticks of greasepaint or other forms of make-up you need. It will also of course tell you how to achieve various effects.

However, before you start turning yourself into a Stage Butler or a Jovial Woman, study the natural contours of your face, and then try to emphasize them by highlighting the prominences and shadowing the hollows, and when you have done that, try to produce the opposite effect. As a simple example, paint a thin line of No. 5 or No. 20 down the centre of your nose and shade the sides with a thinly applied mixture of Nos. 25 and 32; then wipe off the make-up and reverse the process. It is sometimes difficult when you are sitting in front of a mirror to see what effect you have achieved, but by half closing your eyes you will get an impression of what you have done. It helps, when you are applying the make-up, to have a strong light on your face.

The Eyes

Whether or not you use a foundation make-up and whatever you put on in the way of highlights and shadows, you will certainly need to do something about your eyes. Indeed, for some years now, unless playing a character part, the only make-up I have used has been on my eyes. The eyes are the most important part of the actor's face, and even if nature has endowed you with large eyes, fringed by thick dark lashes, you will want to enhance them for work on the stage.

For a basic make-up you will need first to shadow the upper lid. The ladies can probably use their everyday eye shadow for this purpose. For men a purplish colour is probably the best, made from a mixture of dark blue and lake. Blue by itself tends to look effeminate, and lake by itself gives a slightly angry effect. An alternative is dark brown. Colour the lid lightly in the colour you select.

Next you will need a black or very dark brown eyebrow pencil, with which, starting on the side next to the nose, you draw a line on the upper lid as close as possible to the eyelashes. When you reach the last quarter of an inch or so of the eyelid, draw the line away from and above the curve of the lid slightly, and (not too heavily) fill in the gap between the eyelid and your line so that you have a small inverted triangle there, its downward tip coinciding with the corner of the eye, and its upper edge extending slightly beyond it. Draw a similar line about one eighth of an inch below the lashes of the lower lid, following the line of the lashes until just below the centre of the eye or a little beyond, and then drawing the line rather straighter instead of following the curve of the eye, and extending a short way so that it parallels the outer edge of the triangle you have drawn above. These extensions have the effect of lengthening the eye in an outward direction; to compensate and lengthen it in the other direction a small red dot is placed on the nose side of the eye just below the little lump of pink which forms the corner.

The Lips

Most ladies need no instruction in making up their lips. For straight make-ups men should not use any of the red greasepaints on the lips. If you are not using a foundation make-up, you can leave them unpainted, but if you have used a foundation or if you want to alter their shape, the best colour to use is No. 9. Similarly, men should not use carmine on the cheeks, unless deliberately wanting to create a florid effect, and again No. 9 is an appropriate colour to use.

Powder

After you have applied your make-up, you will need to use powder. Theatrical powder is available in many shades, the most usual being Brownish, Rose and Rachel (a pale cream colour). I prefer a mixture of Brownish and Rachel. Whatever colour you use, dab it on firmly and then brush or wipe off the surplus.

Powder has the effect of toning down the make-up you have applied, but this does not mean that you should use a heavy hand in applying your greasepaint, even on the eyes. If you make up your eyes too liberally, especially if you have little make-up on the rest of your face, they will look like two black holes, even after powdering.

Since powder softens the make-up, it is usual to put on the highlights after powdering. Not only does this leave the colours clear, but the slight shine of the make-up in the lights increases the highlighting effect.

During the performance you will probably need to powder again, whenever you have the chance. Stage lighting is usually quite hot and make-up seems to bring out the perspiration, though it affects some actors more than others. I remember a friend of mine playing a scene in *A Bill of Divorcement* in which he stood behind a settee, bending over an actress who had her face turned up towards him. He dripped all over her—so it was perhaps as well that the audience could not see her expression. This actor eventually found that his heavy facial perspiration was helped if he applied an astringent lotion before putting on his make-up.

Character Make-ups

A good book on make-up will give details of all manner of make-ups for various characters. I will confine myself to a few words about ageing.

For the foundation, use No. 6 by itself, or No. 6 with the addition of a little No. 9.

As we get older the flesh on our faces sags and wrinkles, and wrinkles are generally the first thing the actor thinks about when he considers trying to age himself. The question is how to paint on those wrinkles so that they look like wrinkles. Again it's a matter of shadows and highlights. Observe where the wrinkles are on your face; if they are not apparent, frown, laugh, screw up your eyes, do other facial contortions until you can see them. Smooth a narrow band of lake, quite thinly, along the natural lines to create the shadow of an indentation. Then add a very thin line of dark brown or lake in the centre of the band you have painted, actually along the line where your skin creases. Then paint a smooth narrow band of highlight above the band of lake, and powder well (in this case I usually add the highlight before powdering).

A touch of dark blue or purple taken downwards from the inner corners of the eyes, and a highlight smoothed on the flesh below the eye will give you 'bags', while a triangular patch of shadow lightly painted from the jaw line up towards the mouth on either side of the chin will help to give a jowly look. You can add shadows to hollow the temples, and you may also want to use lake as eye shadow and eye liner to give a rheumy look. The lips can be made up with a pale colour, or you can paint them lightly with lake and then place lines of white on them from the inside towards the front to give them a wrinkled effect.

If the hair is to be whitened (see below), brushing the eyebrows against the direction in which they lie with a stick of white greasepaint will not only whiten them, but leave them with a spiky appearance which also suggests age.

Hair

I am never quite sure whether hair should come under make-up or costume. It can certainly be part of the costume, and if an actor does not know how to dress his hair for a particular period, the wardrobe mistress may need to show him how to do so. Hair lacquers are obviously of great assistance in keeping the hair in position.

The most effective way of changing the hair colour is of course to have it professionally dyed, but few amateurs will wish to go that far. Some of the colour rinses on sale are quite effective, and can be washed out afterwards.

For white or greying hair sprays are available or you can powder the hair with talc or starch, remembering to apply it evenly and at the same time as sparingly as possible. It is best used on slightly greasy hair to which it will cling. If your hair is dry and especially if you have been too lavish with the starch, you are likely to envelop yourself in a white cloud every time you move your head sharply. White greasepaint can be used on the hair at the temples or to produce streaks in the hair, but if you are going to do this look carefully at people whose hair is naturally white in these places and try to reproduce that appearance. White hair does not usually grow in a small hard-edged patch. Yet again, the advice is to apply the make-up lightly, and especially avoid plastering the hair down with it.

Wigs

Wigs can be hired. A few years ago wigs for ladies were very fashionable and some of these may be available for use in plays, though they are usually elaborately and permanently curled, and it is much better to have a straight-haired wig which can be set as desired (though you may need the services of a professional hairdresser to get it looking really right).

Before you put a wig on, you need to get your own hair out of the way by brushing it flat, or if it is long by binding it as tightly as you can to your skull. It's not very comfortable, but you have to suffer for your art, as they say.

Professional wigs often have a 'forehead' of cloth, which is usually stained a dark brown after years of application of make-up, and it is very difficult for amateurs, who will not be using heavy make-up, to disguise this. Especially hard to get rid of is the line where the false forehead finishes, but sometimes it can be hidden by painting a wrinkle there.

Wigs need to be treated with great care, and it is a good thing to have wig stands (polystyrene ones are usually readily available) on which they can be placed after the performance. Always take them off and put them on carefully so as not to disturb the setting of the hair.

Beards and Moustaches

Beards and moustaches of all shapes and colours can be purchased, and they usually come with a small backing of fabric to which the hair is attached. They are fixed to the face with spirit gum. Spirit gum stings and many amateur actors prefer Copydex, but I have never found it at all satisfactory for made-up beards and moustaches—it doesn't give a strong enough adherence, and it also gets into the hairs of the piece and makes them messy. It does work quite well, however, with crêpe hair, to which we will come in a moment.

To apply a made-up moustache or beard, clean the appropriate area of skin of the make-up you have already applied, paint the skin and the fabric of the hair-piece with spirit gum, and when they have both become tacky, place the piece in position, stretching the skin as you do so. Have a damp cloth by you and press the piece with it against your face firmly for a minute or so. Since moustaches and beards have a nasty habit of coming unstuck, have a bottle of spirit gum and your damp cloth in some handy place in the wings so that you can carry out emergency repairs. If your moustache or beard comes unstuck while you are on stage, firm pressure will sometimes put it back in place temporarily, but a new application of gum is really the only answer.

Made-up moustaches normally come in one piece, but I have found that I am in less danger of them coming loose, especially in a singing part for which the lips stretch more than in ordinary speech, if I cut the moustache carefully in half down the centre, and apply the two pieces separately. Of course, one has to ensure that both sections go on at the same angle.

Crêpe Hair

Many amateurs still use crepe hair, though it has largely gone out of favour in the professional theatre. Crêpe hair is available in a large variety of shades, but it is nevertheless often difficult to get it to look the same colour as your own natural hair; to do so, you may need to use more than one shade of crepe hair or alter the colour by the use of greasepaint or powder.

Crêpe hair comes in a tightly plaited braid, and when you unravel it, is very crinkly. Sometimes it can be used satisfactorily in this condition, but if you want to straighten it you can do so by soaking it in hot water and then wrapping it tightly around something (a milk bottle would do) while it dries. Before you use it, tease it out a bit with your fingers.

To make a beard from crêpe hair you do not glue one long length of it to your face, but take a number of short lengths and gum them on one at a time, starting from the chin and working towards the line of your own hair by your ears, gradually building up the beard. Remember that beards grow under the jaw line and chin, so the hair must be applied there too. Similarly, a moustache is built up from several small pieces of crêpe hair stuck on in a downward direction, rather than with a long piece glued across the upper lip. When the beard or moustache has been applied (and the technique with the spirit gum is the same as already described), trim the crêpe hair with scissors, shaping it so that you get the effect you want. Crêpe hair goes a long way, and it is a good idea to practise at home. Your first results may seem discouraging, but you will probably soon get the hang of it.

When you have put on a wig or a beard or a moustache, whether using made-up pieces or crêpe hair, you will often find that the edges look far too hard and sharply defined. You can use small pencil strokes of an appropriately coloured make-up to soften the line. The edges of wigs, incidentally, may need to be fixed down with spirit gum.

If you do not clean made-up moustaches or beards after use, you will find when you come to use them again that the gauze backing is stiff with dried spirit gum. Tease them gently in your fingers, and the spirit gum will turn to dust and flake off.

Nose Putty

Nose putty is a very useful accessory, a small amount of which, if judiciously used, can quite transform your appearance. It is really like a sort of plasticine. Work a small piece in your fingers until it is soft, press it on to your nose and mould it to the desired shape, smoothing it down at the edges so that it almost blends into your skin. It will probably adhere quite satisfactorily by itself, but you can use spirit gum to fix it securely. I have found that it makes my nose perspire, and that it is worth taking it off and re-applying it during an interval. Once you have fixed the putty in place you will have to apply make-up to cover it and the surrounding flesh so that all are of the same colour.

Black Eyes

Surprisingly large numbers of plays seem to call for one or more of the characters to appear with a black eye. This does not mean that you should cover your eye and the eye hollow with black or dark brown make-up. Black eyes aren't black at all—the bruise shows a mixture of colours in which purple and pale yellow predominate, and they don't have a hard edge. The next time you see someone in real life with a black eye, take a note of exactly what it looks like. The same advice applies to scars.

Blacked-out Teeth

If you want to appear gap-toothed, you can buy a lacquer to paint on to your teeth, but I have found it works quite well simply to wipe the tooth or teeth dry of saliva and then apply a dark brown or black greasepaint. It feels slightly odd, but it doesn't come off during the performance (just wipe it off afterwards), nor does it taste funny.

Body Make-up

Liquid make-up is available in various shades to cover large areas of the body, and is usually easy to apply, though you may need assistance to get it on evenly in inaccessible places.

If you have to reveal part of your flesh on stage, be careful about any suntan marks, especially the pale strip often left by a wrist-watch. Put a dab of make-up on. And, gentlemen, if you are appearing, let us say, in a play set in ancient Greece, with bare legs, make sure that prior to the performance your every-day socks are not of the kind which will leave the mark of their elasticated tops.

Ladies used to apply something called 'wet-white' to prevent their skin, especially their hands, from looking red under the heat of stage lighting. Happily, the various body make-ups on the market have replaced wet-white.

Taking Off Make-up

Remove any false hair—gently if it is a made-up piece, because you will want to use it again—and give your face a quick wipe over with a tissue, which will remove quite a lot of the make-up. Then take a fair quantity of removal cream and rub it all over your face and any other areas where you have used make-up; this will not only loosen the make-up but also any spirit gum on your skin. Wipe off the resulting yukkiness with a tissue or an old towel or face-cloth, after which, in my experience, there is nothing to beat a good scrubbing with plenty of soap and hot water. Make sure that you get rid of all the greasepaint, which may otherwise clog the pores and produce spots.

If you have your own make-up kit it is usually in a bit of a mess after a show, and it is worth taking the time to tidy it up, sharpen the eyebrow pencils, and note anything that you will need to replace before the next play.

12

Properties

Most acting editions of plays include a list of properties, but they are not always complete nor detailed enough, and the person in charge of props should read the play carefully, making a list of everything that is required, including not only the articles which will be used, but also those which will be wanted to dress the stage. Having done so, ask the director for an opportunity to talk to the cast at one of the early rehearsals to see whether any of them can provide any of the articles needed. Ask to see everything that members of the cast promise to provide long before the dress rehearsal, especially if it is a period play, because the properties must look right, and you may need time to find an alternative for something unsuitable. You will probably need to research into the period and look at books and paintings to be sure of accuracy. On the other hand, though the more authentic in appearance the better, your props don't have to be antiques, and few in your audience will be expert enough to know the exact dates of the various pieces.

Of course, it is more than likely that the cast will not be able to supply all the props needed, and it will be necessary either to make or hire some of them. Most groups have members or friends who will be willing to have a shot at making properties, and it is sometimes surprising what wonderful things they can produce out of unlikely materials. Do make sure, however, before anyone starts work on the manufacture of a prop that they know exactly what is wanted, what size it has to be, and how it will be used.

During rehearsals you will probably not use the correct properties, especially if any have to be hired, but it is very important that substitute props should be provided for the use of the actors as soon as they have been able to dispense with their books. It does not matter whether the understudy prop is much like the final article will be, provided that it is roughly the same shape and size. Any old crockery will do duty for the best china or glass; rolled up newspaper can be used for anything from flowers to a rolling pin to swords.

For the dress rehearsal and performances, properties divide into three groups: personal properties—those which the actors have about their persons, which 'belong' to them, and which they carry on stage themselves; non-personal properties—articles such as a tea trolley, which are brought on during the action; and stage properties—those which are on stage at the beginning of the scene, including those which are there solely as part of the setting and are not moved or used during the play. All these have to be checked before the performance begins and at the start of each scene. Although the stage manager is finally responsible for seeing that everything on stage is ready for the curtain-up, the person in charge of props must be sure that everything in his department is ready and in place. At the risk of upsetting the actors, I would suggest that when you check their personal props you ask to see them rather than being content with the mere assurance that they have them. For the remainder, you will need a table on which you can lay the properties out, and to which the actors know that they will come to collect them or return them if they carry them off stage. If you have many small props to deal with, it helps to cover the table with plain paper and write on it the names of the props in the position that they will always occupy on the table.

After the last performance you will need to check that all properties which have been borrowed or hired are returned to their owners. Keep those that have been specially made—they may be useful again in some other play.

Valuables

Valuable properties are a nuisance, and the greatest care has to be taken with them. If the prop concerned belongs to one of the cast, it is probably best for that person to take it home after each performance, but you had better have a substitute to hand, however inadequate, in case the owner forgets to bring it the next night. If a valuable property has been borrowed from someone other than a member of the cast or stage staff, the property manager will have to look after it himself. Apart from the possibility of theft, heirlooms and antiques are singularly liable to damage; insurance should be taken out, which is another reason for rejecting offers of such items if it is possible to do without them.

Disposable Properties

Properties that are destroyed or otherwise disposed of during the performances will have to be replaced. Make sure that the drinks bottles have been topped up, that the cigarette box has been filled, and that papers which get torn up during the play have been replaced. Sometimes an ornament or something of the kind has to be broken during the action of the play. Nothing is likely to cause the actors more dismay and the audience more amusement than when it is hurled to the floor only to bounce and fail to shatter. Break a suitable ornament beforehand and glue it lightly together. If you have several performances, you may prefer to prepare several vases or whatever they are in advance, rather than have to stick the same one together between each performance.

Letters

A careful property manager will make at least two copies of any letters or documents that are used in a play—papers often get crumpled or lost. If an actor has to read aloud from, say, a letter, even though he should know the contents by heart, the letter should be written out in full so that he can actually read it.

Flowers

In the professional theatre real flowers on the stage are supposed to be unlucky. Amateurs generally do not seem to be bothered by this superstition. But do make sure that your flowers are appropriate for the time of year in which the scene takes place. If you do not want to use real flowers or they are not available, you can use plastic or paper imitations, though they should be non-inflammable. Foliage can usually be found, but in winter you may need to make paper leaves to fix to a branch or twig.

Paintings

Paintings are often needed in plays. If they are used only as dressing for the stage, it is usually possible to borrow something suitable, but if they have to be of a specific subject—perhaps a portrait of the heroine—you will have to find a tame artist who can produce something which will look right. It is worth going to some trouble to get a really capable painter rather than leaving it to a member of your group who, though willing, is not talented enough.

Mirrors, Pictures and Spectacles

Mirrors and the glass of pictures have an unfortunate habit of reflecting the lighting, which can be very unpleasant for the audience. A light film of grease or soap will solve the problem. Remove the glass from pictures if you can. For the same reason, if spectacles have to be worn by the actors, it is preferable to have empty frames. Actors who cannot normally see without their glasses should learn the play well enough to do without them (after all, there are several successful amateur groups whose members are blind), or should wear contact lenses.

Suitcases

Put something in suitcases so that they look appropriately heavy.

Food and Drink

Food which has to be eaten on the stage has to meet two requirements: the first and more important is that it should be very easy to eat; the second is that, if visible to the audience, it should look reasonably like what it is meant to be. Mashed potatoes (and indeed any mashed or puréed vegetable), scrambled egg, soft banana—these are the kinds of food that slip down easily, and can be disguised with gravies, thin sauces and culinary colourings. If the food is meant to be hot, try to have it so, especially if it is served on stage from vegetable or chafing dishes—it is nice to see steam when the lid is raised. Cut bread and butter very thin and remove the crusts. Sandwiches need not contain any filling (but if you want to make sure that the audience sees the cucumber in the sandwiches in *The Importance of Being Earnest*, put very thin segments of cucumber around the edges of the sandwiches). Whatever you give the cast to eat, do make sure that they know in advance what it is.

The same applies to drinks. Tea and coffee can be real—audiences like to see real hot tea come out of the teapot. By the way, put small paper coasters in the saucers for the cups to rest on—it stops them from rattling in the hands of nervous actors. Alcoholic drinks must not be real. Gin or vodka can of course be water, while the standard substitute for whisky and brandy is cold tea (though water coloured with burnt sugar can be used). When pouring the cold tea into an empty whisky or brandy bottle or decanter, do so slowly and gently, for otherwise a long-lasting head of bubbles may form, and whatever else it may look like, it will certainly not resemble a spirit. Some groups use Ribena for red wine or port, but to my mind it rarely looks right, and I prefer water appropriately tinted with culinary colouring. Lucozade is often used for white wine, but it is rather too yellow, and its sparkle is usually inappropriate. Very weak lime juice is better. Champagne is a real problem, especially if the bottle has to be opened on stage, when you will probably have to use one of the mock champagnes (much cheaper than the real thing), keeping the label away from the audience's sight; if the champagne bottle has been opened off stage, you can probably get away with an appropriately coloured fizzy soft drink. Beer is difficult to fake, but should be less dangerous from the point of view of inebriating the cast, and in any case it is possible nowadays to obtain non-alcoholic beer.

Candles and Lamps

Many local regulations ban the use of candles or lighted oil lamps on the stage. It is possible to make a 'candle' from a tube of white paper concealing a torch battery, with a switch on the candlestick, the bulb at the top of the tube being disguised by a wisp of tissue paper (fireproofed) in the shape of a flame and suitably coloured. Oil lamps which are in fact worked by electricity are fairly readily obtainable.

Cigarettes

Remember, if you are presenting a play which takes place before World War II, that cigarettes then were not king size and were rarely cork-tipped.

Lighters often become temperamental when appearing before an audience, and you should place boxes of matches on stage as understudies for them. Leave one match sticking out of the box, which makes it easier for the actor to find with his nervous fingers. Also place plenty of good-sized, heavy ashtrays on the stage, preferably deep rather than shallow, since they should be partially filled with damp sand, which will extinguish a cigar or cigarette safely and quickly.

Rain and Snow

If a character has to come on stage in clothes which are wet from rain, he may of course be able to get the effect by standing outside the theatre or hall if it is raining at the time (and it usually is). Alternatively, have a watering can of water to pour over the unfortunate actor. Do so from a height, and make sure that the water which does not fall on the actor will not damage anything or make the floor slippery.

Snow on the shoulders of characters can be simulated with coarse salt, but if the actors are to stay in their outside clothes for any length of time, they will have to be told to brush the salt off themselves while on stage, since of course it will not melt as snow would.

Snow falling on the stage may be the responsibility of the stage manager rather than the props person. If you have no height above your stage it may be difficult to use the technique of dropping tiny scraps of paper or small pieces of polystyrene from above, which you do by having it in a container such as a sheet with small holes in it, which is suspended above the stage and from which the snow falls when the container is agitated by an off stage rope. Much ingenuity is needed. Failing that, since throwing handfuls of 'snow' from the wings doesn't look at all right, the best thing is to hand the problem to the lighting department, who can obtain a continuous slide which will give the effect of snow from a projection lantern.

Guns

Some toy guns look authentic, but of course if they have to be fired on stage an appropriate offstage sound effect will have to be synchronized to the firing. Old-fashioned guns—muskets, flintlocks and the like—can be hired, and so can practical guns, together with blank cartridges. If using a revolver, load all the chambers with blanks in case one fails to fire. Make sure that you and the actor using the gun both know exactly how to load and fire it. You will need a licence for a practical gun, even if it is specially made so that it fires blanks only—apply to a Police Station for a form and send it in well in advance of the production.

13

Publicity, Box Office and Front of House

Publicity

How do you get an audience for your play? Obviously you have to tell people about it. You can do so by means of advertisements in the Press (including perhaps the local parish magazine), but this may prove expensive. You can have posters printed for the members of your society to display in their windows, but if you intend also to persuade local shop-keepers to take posters it is as well to keep them fairly small (probably not more than 200mm × 300mm). Posters too are costly to produce, and though it is certainly important to have some notices of your production available for the general public to see, it may be preferable to have a few hand-lettered ones only, provided of course that you have someone in your group who can produce a legible and attractive article.

If you think it worth it, you could also have handbills printed—perhaps sufficient for every house in the neighbourhood to receive one, and you might be able to arrange with a friendly newsagent for them to be delivered with the papers, or you could get your members to plod round the streets popping them in letter-boxes.

Keep the information on posters and handbills to the minimum: the name of your group, the title and author of the play, the venue, dates and times of performances, the prices of tickets and where they may be obtained. The less wording you include, the cheaper the printing and the more easily read the notices will be.

Or you may, over a period of time, build up a mailing list of patrons who will be likely to come to your play if given the chance of ordering tickets. It often works quite well, but of course there is again the question of expense, even if you send out no more than a duplicated letter.

It is sometimes possible to obtain free publicity in advance from your local Press, but in most cases they will be looking for something more than a mere announcement that you are producing a play on such and such a date. You need to give them 'a story'—'Seventy-five-year-old treads the boards', 'His leading lady—actors announce their engagement', 'The armour-knitters of Ambridge'. Headlines like that may sound corny, but most local newspapers would give you a few column inches for such stories, and maybe even a photograph.

Free publicity is fine, but unless you have a long-established reputation for excellence, or if perhaps you perform in a local theatre which has its regular patrons, you will probably find that any expenditure on publicity is hardly covered by the number of tickets you sell as a result of it. The fact of the matter is that most of the audience for an amateur show come because members of the society have sold tickets to their relations, friends and acquaintances. It is often very difficult nowadays to persuade people to leave their homes and the television on a winter's night to sit in a draughty hall and watch an amateur production. The best way of doing so is by direct personal contact, and even then you may have to be very persuasive and persistent.

Tickets

You will need to have tickets printed, and it is usual to include on them the name of the society, the title of the play and often the author's name, the venue, date and time of the performance, and the price. Some companies do not number their tickets, and work on the basis that the first comers among the audience can choose their own seats. More usually the seats are numbered as well as reserved, and the seat numbers will have to be written on the tickets (normally it is much too expensive to have them printed on). If you are presenting your play more than once and if you are charging different prices, it will save printing costs to have all the dates and prices printed on all the tickets (for example, 'Thursday 10th March, Friday 11th March, Saturday 12th March—£1.50, £1, 75p') and then cross out those bits which do not apply.

It helps the box office to have different colour tickets for the different nights of performance, and for different prices too. It is of course much simpler to charge the same price for all seats, but you may wish to make a reduction for those at the back of the hall, or to vary the prices for the different days of perform- ance, or to have reduced prices for children or pensioners. You will have to make your own decision about the prices, but don't be afraid to charge a reasonable amount. Generally speaking, amateurs pitch their ticket prices at figures which are very low indeed compared to the price of seats in the profes- sional theatre. On the other hand, unless you can offer your audience not only a near-professional standard of production, but also the comfort and good sight-lines of a professional theatre, you must beware of putting up the prices to a point where they will discourage people from coming.

It is possible of course to duplicate your tickets instead of having them printed. Some groups use their programmes as tickets, which means that everyone has one, and any revenue lost on the sale of programmes may be made up by not having to print separate tickets.

Programmes

You will need to have a programme printed or duplicated. It should carry the name of the company, the title of the play and author's name, the cast list and the names of all the behind- scene helpers, a synopsis of scenes (where and when the various acts and scenes of the play take place) and probably some indication of when the intervals will be and how long they will last and whether refreshments will be served during them. You may also wish to include some expression of thanks for the use of the hall, and you may have to print a statement about safety regulations if the local licensing authority requires it.

Some groups like also to include a short paragraph about the play, or perhaps a list of their previous productions, or an appeal for new members, but it has to be borne in mind that the more printed matter your programme contains, the higher the printer's bill will be. For this reason too it is often doubtful whether advertisements in the programme will be of much benefit to you. Advertisements can usually be obtained only from local shopkeepers, who have little expectation of gaining much from them, look upon the cost as a charity donation, and are therefore not over inclined to pay what they may consider an exorbitant sum, though in fact it is little more than the printer's charge to you. If you do decide to sell advertising space in your programme, make sure what the cost of setting the ads will be, so that you fix the price of the space accordingly and don't end up out of pocket.

People coming to see an amateur show do not usually expect to pay much for the programme, so price it to make a profit if you can, but certainly not a large one. At the same time, it is worth making the programme as attractive as you can afford to do, for it helps to give a good first impression.

The Box Office

I would suggest that the front of house manager should take overall responsibility for box office arrangements, though he may wish to delegate the job. Whoever is going to be in charge of it, he will need, if the tickets are numbered, to have a chart of the seating arrangements for each performance, so that tickets sold can be crossed off on it and new customers can see what is still available.

Some societies appoint one or two persons from among their members to look after the box office, whereas others persuade a local shop to handle ticket sales for them. The disadvantage of the former method may be that, if the box office manager is at work during the day, he will be available for ticket sales only in the evenings and at weekends, but equally the shop will not be selling tickets after closing for the evening and they will not be available at rehearsals.

Since it is primarily the cast and others connected with the production who sell tickets, I think it is sensible for the box office representative to attend all rehearsals during, say, the last two or three weeks before the show. If you do nevertheless choose to put your tickets on sale through a local shop, you may wish to have an evening before you do so when the cast has the opportunity of buying tickets. This sometimes causes complaints because they have taken all the best seats, but since they are the prime ticket sellers, this seems to me not unreasonable.

The box office manager may have to give priority to certain persons, such as the society's president or patrons. It should also be his responsibility to get in touch with the local Press, assuming that you want a report of your production to appear in the local paper, to arrange when their critic will attend and to keep a ticket or tickets for him.

Needless to say, the box office manager needs to be a methodical person, capable of keeping clear records and of handling fairly large sums of money. He may also have to be something of a credit controller. In some societies it is customary to charge everyone as soon as they take the tickets, but in other cases the cast and stage staff may be allowed credit until they have collected the cash from the eventual purchasers. It is good to have the money in straight away, but there are advantages in the credit system, particularly since amateur audiences often change their minds and return tickets or want to change them.

The Theatre or Hall

Unless you are lucky enough to have a permanent little theatre of your own or are performing in a professional theatre, you will probably be using a church or village hall, and the front of house manager should check some weeks before the first performance that the booking is firm and that other regular users of the hall have been informed that it is not available to them on the nights of the dress rehearsals and performances. It should be the job of the hall manager to do this, but you may find that he leaves it to you. There is little worse than to arrive for the first performance to find that a badminton club has angrily moved all your carefully prepared seats and is playing a match.

Few small halls nowadays have a resident caretaker who will set out the chairs for you, so the front of house manager will probably have to do the job himself, possibly with a team of helpers. When you apply for the licence to put on a public presentation, you should find out from the local authority whether there are any regulations to be observed concerning the number of chairs you can use, whether they have to be fixed together in some way, whether there are rules about the width of gangways, and so on. It is of course important to find out these details before the seating charts are drawn up.

If you have not performed in the hall before, you should check the sight-lines. Very often it is impossible to see much from the sides of the front two or three rows, and so you may have fewer seats in these rows. If there is room, it is a good idea to stagger the rows so that the seats are not directly behind each other, which helps visibility a great deal if the audience is on a flat floor. Don't place the seats too close together, unless fire regulations demand that they should be linked—the more comfortable your audience is, the better they will enjoy the play.

The seats and rows will probably need to be numbered and lettered. You may be able to fasten labels on the seats with sellotape, or chalk the row letters on the floor, but be careful not to do anything which will damage the equipment of the hall, and remember that you will have to remove any signs, notices, marks and so on at the end of the last performance.

Many halls in which amateurs perform are somewhat un-attractive places. You can make them look more pleasant with flowers or other decorations. Photographs of the society's previous productions could be displayed. If you have any choice in the matter, do see that the hall is well lit for the audience before and after the play and during the intervals.

Smoking.   Nowadays audiences accept the fact that they will not be allowed to smoke in the auditorium of a professional theatre, and most amateur groups are following suit. A couple of 'No Smoking' signs will do the trick. Smokers will have to go outside during an interval for their quick drag.

The Dressing-Rooms

The front of house manager should also take responsibility for the dressing-room or rooms. Even in these days when there is little false modesty around, it is preferable to have one room for the men and another for the women in the cast, and indeed in some areas the licensing authorities insist on this, though I have never been able to understand what business it is of theirs whether members of the cast see those of the opposite sex in various stages of undress, which is hardly likely in the circumstances to lead to licentious behaviour. However, even if you cannot manage separate dressing-rooms, you might consider dividing the one room by hanging a curtain across it. If any member of the cast does have to strip to the skin, there is usually a toilet available.

If you are lucky, your dressing-room will be amply provided with hooks for clothes. If not, then see if you can borrow or buy cheaply one of those racks on castors which are used in dress shops. If at all possible, supply a chair for each member of the cast—somewhere for them to put their belongings and sit if they want to.

At least one good-sized mirror is essential in the dressing-room, and if you can provide a table with mirrors and good lighting, it will be much appreciated by the actors when they put on their make-up. Indeed, you may think it worthwhile to get your friendly carpenter and electrician to rig up a mirror or mirrors surrounded by light bulbs, such as the professionals use.

Looking after the Public

The front of house manager will have to find a team to help with showing people to their seats, selling programmes, providing and selling refreshments and sweets, and he may appoint someone to be in charge of each of these activities.

Refreshments. Audiences at plays like to have refreshments during the interval. If you put your play on in a professional theatre there will probably be a bar, and you will have no problems because the theatre staff will run it. It is more likely that you will be in a small hall and will be serving tea or coffee (preferably not both, which makes life too complicated, though you may wish to add a cold drink to the menu). It's a nuisance in many ways, but it usually makes a profit.

The front of house manager will have to arrange for sufficient people to be on duty to prepare the tea or coffee and to buy the ingredients. If you are fortunate, there may be a large room near to the auditorium to which the audience can come for refreshments. If not, the front of house manager will have to arrange for distributors too, making sure that trays are available.

The tea or coffee makers will want to know when the interval will come, so that their brew will be ready on time. The front of house manager should be able to get this information from the stage manager. The kitchen staff will also like to have some idea of how many cups they will have to serve. I think one of the best ways of doing this is to get the programme sellers to ask members of the audience as they come in whether they want tea in the interval; if they do, the programme seller can take their money and give them a cloakroom ticket which can later be exchanged for the cup. While the first act is on you can see how many tickets have been sold and prepare accordingly, adding a few extra for those who didn't buy tickets but have now changed their minds.

If you have more than one interval, you will have to decide whether to serve refreshments in more than one of them. If you ask me, once is enough, and the other interval(s) can be cut to the length of time needed for the scene and costume changes.

There are problems with refreshments at amateur shows. One is the collection of empties if the audience is served in the auditorium. Obviously the performance cannot continue until this is done, or until the audience has returned if the refreshments are served in another place, and the stage manager will have to hold the curtain until the front of house manager gives the all clear.

The other principal difficulty is that the tea ladies usually have very penetrating voices and are not easy to keep quiet, and that washing up is never a silent process. If the noise of clattering cups and saucers can be heard in the auditorium, leave the washing up until the show is over. This may mean that the cast and stage staff have to do it themselves because the tea ladies have gone home, but that is the lesser evil.

The front of house manager should arrange for tea to be sent round for the cast and stage staff at the very beginning of the interval.

If you are intending to sell alcoholic drinks, you will have to apply for a licence to do so, unless the hall already has one.

Insurance

Most halls carry insurance against accidents to members of the audience and to the cast and stage staff while they are in the building, but you should check on the scope of the policy. You may want to add cover for your scenery, costumes and any other property which belongs to your society, including personal possessions, and you can also insure against having to cancel the show at a late stage for any reason.

14

The Performance

The Director

His job is finished now, and he must hand over to the stage manager. If he thinks of giving any instructions to the cast, he should avoid the temptation, and unless there has been some last-minute disaster, should confine himself to wishing them luck (or perhaps to saying, 'Break a leg!', following the odd theatrical tradition that it is unlucky to wish actors good luck). At the most he might tell them to go out and enjoy themselves. If he is both director and stage manager, then he must act only as the latter.

This does not mean, of course, that he cannot watch each performance. Indeed, he should—if only because his known presence in the audience may prevent any undisciplined or over-enthusiastic members of the cast from improvising or experimenting to the detriment of the production. He may also want to take notes and give them to the cast between performances, but I think he should restrict himself to really essential comments, and should try to be aware of whether the individual actors will be responsive and capable of carrying out his instructions, or whether his notes will simply confuse them and make them more nervous.

The Stage Manager

The stage manager has responsibility for everything that happens back stage during the performance. Before the curtain goes up on any scene, he must satisfy himself that the cast is ready to come on, and in the correct costumes, that all the scenery and furniture is in position, that properties are ready, that the prompter, lighting and sound staff are all in position, and that the audience is finally seated. If he is lucky he will have a reliable call boy, who can take over some of these jobs, but the responsibility remains his. He will also control the curtain, ensuring that it is raised, lowered or drawn at exactly the right moment and speed.

It is quite likely that before or during the performance a Fire Officer or some other official will come to inspect the hall and the stage area to assure himself that everything is in accordance with the local regulations. While the front of house manager will accompany him during his inspection of the auditorium, it is the stage manager who will have to stand by with his fingers crossed while a lighted match is applied to the scenery and who will receive the almost inevitable complaints about the clutter in the wing space. Of course, any criticisms that the officer makes have to be taken extremely seriously, and any adjustments that he requires carried out. He has the power to stop the performance, and for this reason it is advisable to study the regulations carefully in advance and adhere to them strictly. Some groups resent these inspections, and one does sometimes feel that they are based on standards which are really intended for the professional theatre rather than for amateurs. You simply have to remember that the regulations are imposed primarily for safety reasons, and the safety of everyone taking part in any way and of the audience is more important than the play.

Fire regulations also usually mean, incidentally, that no smoking is allowed in the back-stage area, and it will be up to the stage manager to see that this rule is not broken.

The Cast

The cast should ideally be present in the theatre or hall or wherever the play is to be performed an hour before curtain up. This is not always possible, but if you are going to be late in arriving, make sure that the stage manager is aware of the fact. Apart from the fact that you will be in no state to act if you have had to scramble into your costume and make-up in a panic, early arrival saves the stage manager from having a heart attack and reassures your fellow actors. Be there early, even if you come, as many amateurs like to do, in full costume and make-up (I have often wondered what the reactions of the police would have been if I had had an accident while driving to a pantomime dressed as the Dame, complete with lipstick, rouge, blue eye-shadow and false eyelashes—no doubt nowadays no one would think it at all strange).

Before the play begins, and particularly before an actor's first entrance, he should remind himself of what he is about to do, what he needs to convey to the audience about himself, about the other actors, about the story of the play. Remember too the need to keep everything fresh, however many times you have performed the play previously—each performance must present the play as though for the first time ever.

If you have the opportunity, check that everything on stage, especially any properties that you will be using, is in its right place (not that you don't trust the stage manager, but it's nice to see for oneself).

It is absolutely vital to stand by for your entrances in good time (not only during the performances, but at rehearsals too). And get yourself into character before you come on.

Nerves. Everyone suffers from nerves before a performance, and even those who appear to be the calmest are probably seething with all kinds of terror inwardly. A certain amount of tension is almost certainly a good thing—if you are too relaxed, you probably won't give a good performance—but nerves can be a serious problem. What, if anything, you do about them depends entirely on you. Some actors leaf frantically through their parts, others pace up and down or chain-smoke or indulge in mild hysterics. I think there are four important rules: check your costume (gentlemen should make sure that their trousers are decently fastened after the obligatory visit to the toilet) and your properties; be certain that you know your first line; respect the manifestation of nerves in other members of the cast and let them get on with whatever they are doing without allowing yourself to be irritated or infected by them; try to control yourself and never ever allow yourself to appear more nervous than you are simply to impress your fellow actors.

The one solution for nerves that I would never recommend is the consumption of alcohol. Some amateurs feel that a stiff brandy will give them courage, and we have all heard stories of the pros who send their dressers out for a couple of bottles of stout. It may be all right for the professionals, but it is my firm opinion that all alcoholic drinks should be banned from the amateur dressing-room and behind the scenes until after the show. Your mind needs to be at its sharpest—not dulled by any so-called 'stimulant'. And if you think one drink doesn't matter, consider how much easier it is to enforce a rule if it is strictly adhered to by all involved. Have as much as you like afterwards—provided that you don't have to drive home.

Audience reactions.   The cast must of course be prepared for all kinds of unexpected noises from the audience, including perhaps a great deal of coughing. Coughing is bad news, meaning not only that several members of the audience have nasty colds, but probably that they, and the healthy ones, are bored. Much more pleasant is laughter or the sound of surprise, but these reactions may often come at moments when you had not expected them; indeed, if you are giving several performances of a comedy, you are likely to find that while the main jokes will get a fairly standard reaction, some of the less obvious lines will be received by different audiences with anything from silence to a loud belly laugh. You have to be ready for whatever comes.

If the audience laughs or if there is any other loud noise, you must wait before speaking the next line, or it will be inaudible. It is usually a bad mistake to wait until the laughter has completely died away, though there may be occasions when it is effective. Try to sense when the laugh is fading and then come in with your line, raising your voice slightly so that you can be heard above the remaining laughter. There may also be times when you need to speak a line (or perhaps the continuation of what you are saying) a moment after the laughter has begun and before it reaches its maximum, and in that way you can build the laugh and make it even bigger. If you do speak through a laugh, either because you forgot to wait for it or perhaps because you were totally unprepared for the audience to find the line funny, then stop and say the line again once the audience has quietened sufficiently. If you are fairly experienced you may be able to help a beginner who has spoken his line through a laugh by asking, 'What did you say'—but some novices may of course be stunned into total paralysis by such an improvisation.

Don't kill laughs by distracting the audience's attention with movements. Wait until they are ready for you.

If you are doing a good job you will probably experience that marvellous rapport which flows in both directions from actor to audience and from audience to actor. It is a wonderful feeling to have the audience in the palm of your hand, and it provides the stimulus for an actor to produce his best performance.

When things go wrong. If you dry (forget your lines), don't ever say, 'Sorry!', and don't turn towards the prompter with a beseeching look. Just listen for the prompt and try to pick up the speech as soon as you can. If you can't hear the prompter, it is sometimes possible to move over to the side of the stage where she is, but try to do so as though you would have moved there anyway and without making it obvious what you are doing. If your fellow actor dries, you may be tempted to whisper his line out of the corner of your mouth (the upstage corner of course!). This can help sometimes, but more often than not it makes the fault more noticeable to the audience, who may actually hear you, so leave prompts to the prompter.

The biggest problem with drying is that very often you are convinced that it is your fellow actor who is at fault, not you. If there is a pause, never be complacent, and listen especially carefully to the prompter in case it is your line that she is saying. The more familiar you are with the play, the easier it will be when it comes to a dead halt for you to recognize what has happened, and that may enable you to get it back on the rails.

Supposing someone is late on his entrance. You can try to cover the pause by ad-libbing, if your mind works quickly enough. Don't cast panicky looks off stage, which will make it crystal clear to the audience that something is sadly amiss. If nothing else occurs to you, stay silent, still in character, and pray, both for the missing actor to arrive quickly and for the audience to believe that the pause is intended.

All sorts of others unfortunate things can happen—guns fail

to fire, vital props are missing, the curtain sticks, bits of the scenery fall down, costumes disintegrate, moustaches come unstuck. You will find these and many other horrors discussed in that splendid book, *The Art of Coarse Acting* by Michael Green, together with various solutions to the problems, most of which simply made the situation worse. It is impossible to give specific advice for disasters, because whether or not they can be overcome depends so much on circumstances and the abilities of individual actors. All one can say is that the calmer you remain, the more likely you are to be able to cope. Reassure yourself with the curious fact that although audiences are very quick on the uptake and you should never underrate their capacity for noticing small details, they are not always aware of things that go wrong. Perhaps they believe it all to be part of the play, or unconsciously they bring down a kindly shutter over their critical faculties in these cases, or maybe they are simply as good at acting as those on the stage when it comes to a friendly white lie about not having seen anything untoward.

Whatever goes wrong, try to avoid inquests in the dressing-room afterwards, or at least keep them amicable. The culprit is probably feeling awful anyway, and you won't help his future performances by bitter recriminations.

I suppose the worst crisis occurs when someone in the cast is suddenly taken seriously ill just before or during the performances, or even dies. The theatre tradition is of course that the show must go on, and even in the event of a death you may be justified in saying, 'Poor So-and-so would have hated the play to be cancelled.' But few amateur groups have the luxury of understudies, and if there is no time for anyone else to learn the lines, the only course is to send someone on with a book to read the part. This may be a job for the director, or perhaps for the prompter—wherever possible choose someone who has been intimately connected with the production and is familiar not only with the lines but with the moves too.

Destroying the illusion. One of the minor penalties of taking part in a play is that you can't see it from the auditorium. Some amateurs, if they are off stage for long enough, will go round to the back of the hall to watch, while still in their costumes and make-up. This should be absolutely taboo. I don't suppose it is ever possible to stop the actors, again still dressed for the play, from greeting their friends and relations after the show, but I would much prefer it if they would change back into their everyday clothes first. You should never destroy the illusion that there is a different world up there on the stage, peopled by characters who exist only in that other world.

You should also avoid peeping between the curtains before the play or during an interval. In most amateur halls it is almost impossible to do so without the audience being aware of you.

Another vital rule is that silence must be kept behind scenes, apart of course from any dialogue or noises which are meant to be 'off'. Whispering in the wings can be most disturbing to those on stage, and is sometimes audible to the audience. I remember one occasion when the audience distinctly heard one actor tell another to go to hell just before his entrance. The fact that it was a Nativity play added, alas, to the amusement. Sometimes the dressing-rooms are in close proximity to the stage and it is very difficult to keep silent there, but somehow it must be done.

The Curtain Call

At the end of the play the cast will take one or more curtain calls. They should have been rehearsed in them, but it is the stage manager who has to decide when to pull the curtain, how many calls to take and how long each of them should be. He should have firm instructions from the director about how many calls he should give—usually two will suffice, unless the audience is particularly enthusiastic. Try to keep as small a gap as possible between the end of the play and the first curtain call, or the audience's applause may peter out, which is embarrassing for everyone.

Some societies like to bring on the director, or if they are a church group may expect their minister to appear and make a short speech. My own preference is for no one but the cast to take the applause and for no speeches, but I know that different circumstances apply in some companies.

At the curtain call the practice is sometimes observed of giving bouquets to the ladies of the cast. Personally, I am very much against this, unless it is very firmly organized by the group itself and only the group's flowers are allowed. The problem is that so often the person playing a tiny, almost non-speaking role is the one who gets the biggest bouquet, and the leading lady is left with nothing but her own brave smile. It is best, I think, to make it plain that bouquets will not be presented. If the ladies of the cast are aware of this rule they can often head off any admirers and tell them that the thought will be taken for the deed.

Front of House

The front of house staff have the important job of welcoming those who have come to see the play and making them as comfortable as possible. Stewards and programme sellers will have been well briefed beforehand so that they know not only how the rows of seats are numbered and the price of the programme, but also such details as the time the performance will end, whether or not smoking is permitted, the whereabouts of toilets, when and where refreshments will be served. Few amateur groups can offer their audiences cloakrooms, and outdoor coats have to be clutched on knees (if they are not worn to keep the draughts at bay), but if you have such a facility, of course it must be properly manned. Make sure that all front of house staff know where the emergency exits are and what to do if the building has to be evacuated in a hurry.

The theatre or hall will usually be open half an hour before curtain up, and the box office staff will have been present as soon as the public are allowed in. If you are lucky enough to have a large foyer or a separate hall where the audience can gather and perhaps buy sweets and refreshments and (if you have a licence) alcoholic drinks, then it may be worth opening earlier, but on the whole audiences for amateur shows tend to arrive late.

A warning bell should be sounded by the front of house manager before the curtain is due to go up for the first time and at the end of intervals. Whether the bell is sounded once only, three minutes before time, or whether you have further two-and one-minute bells, is a matter of choice. Although it always seems very unprofessional not to start on time, if the audience is still pouring in or if there is still a queue for the interval refreshments, the front of house manager will have to let the stage manager know that the curtain must be delayed.

The National Anthem

Some groups like to play *God Save the Queen* at the beginning or end of each performance. Others have it only on the first or last night. Most companies do not play it at all. If you are going to use it, try to find a record with a minimum of scratches, and play it before the show rather than after. At the beginning it will disturb the audience, but at least they will stay there; at the end, many will simply ignore it.

After the Show

When the audience has gone, there is always a certain amount of clearing up to be done. Many years ago most halls had caretakers who would sweep and clean and make sure that everything was ready for the next performance; nowadays most groups have to do it for themselves. Obvious, you may say, just as it goes without saying that after the last night the scenery has to be taken down and stored and borrowed furniture and props returned, and costumes sorted out and everything tidied. But the point I want to make is that the cast should not consider themselves absolved from such work. Unless you have so many members that there are plenty of people behind the scenes or in front of house to do all that has to be done, there is a job for everyone. If you are an actor, you may like to think of yourself as an Artiste, who has Given his All in the performance and is now drained, utterly exhausted. Yes, but once it's all over, you revert to being an ordinary member of the society, with the same responsibilities as everybody else.

15

Drama Festivals

Festivals are an important part of the amateur drama scene. Many one-act and full-length festivals run for several days or a week or more in the same theatre or hall. In other festivals the competing teams put on the plays as usual in their own venues and an adjudicator visits each of them before announcing the winners. Almost all festivals are in fact competitive, with cups and other awards for the winners and runners-up and sometimes for various other placings such as best actor or best set design.

The Adjudicator

Festivals are usually judged by a professional adjudicator, who is probably a member of the Guild of Drama Adjudicators. He will certainly be an expert—possibly a professional actor, frequently a drama teacher, and will have been through very stringent tests before being accepted as a member of his Guild.

If you have not been to a drama festival you may wonder how he chooses between the various productions. Only very rarely is there a set play which all the competing groups have to perform. Usually the adjudicator is faced in a week with six different full-length plays or twenty or more one-acters. He has a marking system to help him, the standard arrangement being 40 marks for acting, 35 for production (direction), 10 for stage presentation and 15 for dramatic achievement, making a total of 100. Some festivals give marks for choice of play, which is more often a question of the suitability of the play to the company performing it than of its quality as a play, though adjudicators always encourage teams to put on well-written plays, and most festivals include at least a sprinkling of the classics. Breaking the plays down into their components in this way allows the adjudicator to compare like and unlike. The marks that he gives normally range between 60 and 90, a spread which the Guild of Drama Adjudicators feels should cover every variation between a poor entry and an excellent one. Many festivals impose penalty marks for infringements of their rules—for instance, if there is a time limit on the length of plays and you have overrun, the adjudicator will be told by the festival organizer how many marks have to be deducted.

Immediately after your performance, or in one-act festivals usually at the end of the evening's programme, the adjudicator will speak to the casts and audience. The oral adjudication will normally cover the same aspects of the production as the marking system, and most adjudicators begin by saying something about the play and its demands (in the case of experimental plays often making some effort to explain what he believes the play to be about, and the playwright's intention), going on to discuss the set, the lighting, the sound, the direction, and the actors, about whom he speaks both as a team and individually, and finishing with a general summing up. There is no need to feel apprehensive. Most adjudicators are kind and helpful, and if yours does criticize you strongly, you probably deserve it, and it may be that he is not pulling his punches because he thinks you are good enough to warrant harsher treatment than he would give to beginners. Don't go away disgruntled, but ask yourself whether he was right, and vow to do better next time.

When, later, you see the marks that the adjudicator has given for your entry, you may find that they do not seem to tie up with the general tenor of his remarks on the evening of your performance. You may have been given what sounded like a 'good' adjudication, yet find yourself near the bottom of the list of marks, or you may have been 'torn to pieces', but highly placed. You will usually be able to tell which teams the adjudicator thinks have done well by the way he speaks about them, but, as I have already suggested, he is likely to be kind in his oral adjudication to the weaker entries, feeling that they need encouragement rather than damnation, and he will be much more critical if your standard is high. Bear in mind too that he speaks extempore and for a limited time, and may not therefore be able to say all that he really intends in the way of praise or blame. He is an experienced professional, and should always get it right (and usually does)—but he is also a human being, not a faultless machine.

Some adjudicators agree to meet the teams or a few of their representatives privately after the public adjudication. It is not intended of course that this should be an argumentative session, with the team disputing the verdict which the adjudicator has given, though a friendly discussion on certain points can take place. Often the teams have questions for the adjudicator, and these interviews can be very helpful.

Some adjudicators offer 'workshop' adjudications, in which they work as director on certain sections of the play, attempting to show how the production could have been improved. This is a very interesting idea and can obviously be of great benefit to the groups involved. The difficulty is in finding time for such work to take place.

You may be offered the opportunity of having a written adjudication on your production. You will have to pay for it, and it will probably contain little that was not said during the oral adjudication, but you may find it useful as a record.

How Are Festivals Run?

The organizing is normally done by a committee of amateur drama enthusiasts who hire the hall or theatre, select the entries, arrange the programme, publicize the festival, sell the tickets and control the finances. They also provide a stage director, some stage hands, a lighting director and front of house staff, though if the festival is to take place in a professional theatre, many of these functions may be carried out by the professional employees. They also of course engage the adjudicator.

Entering Festivals

Most festivals advertise themselves in *Amateur Stage* and tell you where to apply for an entry form. With it you will receive details of the rules, which will cover such matters as the number of participants (many festivals will not accept a cast of less than three), the maximum running time (you will be asked if you are entering a one-act festival to say how long your play will last, which means you probably have to have a read-through before you enter), and will give you information about what stage setting is available and the lighting and other equipment. You will also be asked to submit a copy of the play with your entry; this is for the adjudicator's use, and will be returned to you after the festival.

If your entry is accepted, you will be told when you are to perform. It is sometimes possible to be accepted despite saying that you can only perform on such and such a day, or that your company will not be able to present the play on, for instance, the Friday, but this makes for difficulties in the arrangement of the programme. The festival committee will try to draw up the programme so that it is varied, and so that, in the case of one-act festivals, not all the long-running plays are on the same evening.

You will be asked to provide programme details at quite an early date, and you will be told about the box office arrangements. Any group entering a festival has an obligation to sell tickets for it—a full house each evening not only ensures the financial viability of the festival, but helps the teams, since it is always easier to perform to a large audience than to a mere dozen scattered around the auditorium.

You may be called at some date before the festival for a discussion with the stage director, so that he knows what scenery you are bringing with you, what lighting you require, and so that he can answer your queries, but often you will have only a stage rehearsal period when all these details are settled. For a full-length play, it is usual for the team to set their stage in the morning, then to go through the lighting plot with the festival lighting director, and to spend any time left in rehearsing the cast. With most one-act festivals all this has to be done in a half-hour or so. It sounds fairly terrifying, especially if you do not have a lighting expert in your group and know only that you want the stage to be brightly lit and the cyclorama to give the effect of a summer sky, but you will find that the festival staff is usually extremely helpful and will do everything possible to give you what you want.

If your group has not appeared in the hall or theatre before, it is a good idea to bring the cast with you to this rehearsal, so that they have a brief chance to try out their voices. Besides, you may want them to stand on the stage while you are working out the lighting so that you can see the effect.

At this rehearsal you will probably be told which dressing-room(s) your team will use, what arrangements there are for allowing the team into the auditorium to hear the adjudication, and so on.

The Performance

Although your own stage manager will be in charge during your festival performance, there are some functions which he will probably not be allowed to undertake personally. For instance, it is the festival stage director rather than your stage manager who will decide when the house lights shall go down, and one of the festival staff will probably operate the curtain, being given the cue to do so by your stage manager. In the same way, your lighting director's job will be to give cues for the various changes that have been agreed upon at the stage rehearsal, and he will probably not touch a switch or move a dimmer control himself. Since a certain amount has to be delegated in this way, you may worry that things will go wrong. In a one-act festival the festival stage and lighting staff will be dealing with twenty or more plays, with none of which they are familiar, but they usually take pride in carrying out your wishes perfectly. Minor disasters do occur—lighting changes are slow on cue, the curtain comes a moment before you wanted it, or something of that sort. If the error is a serious one, the festival staff will usually let the adjudicator know that it was their fault rather than yours, and he will not deduct marks for it.

When you come to the evening of the performance, the cast will probably be more nervous than usual. It is not only the thought of performing in a strange hall, but the fact that the adjudicator is out there watching everything with a critical eye. Try to forget it, and just do the best you can. Adjudicators are well used to the problems of festival work and can judge whether something has gone wrong because of the strange conditions and festival nerves, or whether it is a more basic fault in the production. Obviously it is better if you can give a flawless performance, but quite often you will find that the adjudicator makes no mention of that awful moment of silence (which was in any case only a couple of seconds' pause) when everyone forgot their words, or the sound effect which came out too loudly. His job is not to pick up every little detail that he can find to carp about, but to give a more general and constructive criticism.

After the festival performance you will be required to remove all your scenery, props and other equipment from the hall or theatre, which usually means a late night for your team.

The Final Night

At the end of the festival the adjudicator usually gives a brief review of the productions that have been presented, perhaps commenting on the general standards and singling out anything that has particularly pleased him, and then announces which teams have won the various awards. He will not normally give any details of the marks he has awarded—these will be sent to you later.

A good adjudicator is entertaining and at the same time instructive, but naturally those who listen to him do not always agree with what he says, and particularly with his final verdict. Indeed, some festivals have an Audience Award given to the team which gets most votes from those members of the audience who have attended all the performances. The audience votes of course for the play it has most enjoyed, without necessarily considering the technical merit which may have led the adjudicator to a different verdict. I have never been convinced of the value of an Audience Award.

For that matter, the winning or losing of a festival is of little importance. It is very pleasant to be highly praised and to walk away with the premier award, and it is disappointing when you fail, but either way you have to remember that the verdict is no more than one man's opinion, and a different adjudicator might not have made the same decision. Indeed, if you win a first round in the national one-act festival organized by the British Theatre Association (formerly the British Drama League), you will go on to the second round and come up against a different adjudicator who may not be nearly as impressed by your production as the first one was. My group once won a first round with a performance of *The Thirty-Seven Sous of Monsieur Montaudoin*, a farce by Labiche. The adjudicator opened his remarks by describing it as 'a sparkling glass of champagne'. He had criticisms to make, and we tried to follow his advice so that the presentation in the second round was an improvement. But the new adjudicator began by saying in a voice of heavy disapproval, 'This is a foolish, frolicsome French farce,' and we knew at once that we were not going to get anywhere with him.

Yes, of course it is nice to win, and there are some companies which travel round from festival to festival winning cups right, left and centre. Good luck to them. But it isn't really what festivals are about. Even if you are very experienced, it is almost impossible to attend a drama festival without learning something from the adjudicator—something new each time, I mean. And you learn not only from his comments on your own entry, but by watching the other teams and hearing what he has to say about them. Additionally, there is considerable pleasure to be had in trying to anticipate what he will praise, what he will criticize, in thinking out what you would say if you were in his shoes. The more critically and appreciatively you look at others, the more you can benefit yourselves.

And if learning is not sufficient reason for entering a festival, as it should be, then the effort you make to do well certainly is. The company with which I was associated for many years raised its standards very considerably by entering drama festivals regularly. We listened carefully to the various adjudicators we encountered, and tried hard to put into practice the lessons we learned from them. Of course we wanted to win, and were delighted when we did, but I can honestly say that our main objective each time was not the silver cup, but the best performance that we could give.

Some groups enter the same festivals year after year, sometimes regularly carrying off the top award. Do not be put off from entering yourselves because, while such a team is there, you feel you have no chance of winning. They may have a bad year, or may come up against an adjudicator who is not impressed by their particular brand of theatrical expertise. Never say die. In any case, let me repeat that festivals are for enjoyment and for learning, not for winning cups.

Many amateur groups who enter festivals regularly will tell you that there is a great advantage for you if your play is presented on the last night, and that the best position of all in a one-act festival is to be the last play on the last night. There is some truth in this, but little of it is due to any end-of-term feeling on the adjudicator's part. The advantage, if any, comes from the fact that the last night audience is usually the biggest of the week, which helps the teams. Besides, one of the main reasons why a more-than-average number of awards go to the final night entries (and here I am talking of one-act festivals) is often that the festival committee tries to arrange the programme so that some of the most experienced and previously successful teams appear on this night when local dignitaries and celebrities may be present among this their largest audience, and they want to be sure that the entertainment is of a high standard. Some festivals, incidentally, insist that the previous year's winners should, if they enter in the following year, be the first play on.

Even if you have no hope of winning, it is necessary if at all possible for at least one person from your society to attend the last night of the festival when the adjudicator will announce the results. You never know—you might have won something after all. Even if you haven't, the adjudicator might, when he sums up, make additional comments on your production which you will be glad to hear.

If you do win a cup, what will you do with it for the year that it is in your possession? When my group first won a festival we agreed that we would pass the cup around so that every member of the cast and stage staff could have it for a few weeks. Whatever you do with it, remember that whether or not you are entering the festival the next year, any trophies have to be returned in good time for the next presentation.

Choosing a Festival Play

The better the play you choose, the better your chances of doing well in a festival, and a really well written play is usually easier to direct and act in, and more enjoyable for all concerned, than something of poor quality. However, really good plays can make demands beyond the capacity of the company, and you have to consider that aspect. Festivals are sometimes won by trite, poorly written plays which have been brilliantly presented. Another point to bear in mind is that the smaller your cast, the higher the standard of acting that will be required of them. Most one-act festivals will accept excerpts from full-length plays, but do make sure if you decide to enter one act of a full-length play that it will be intelligible to the audience.

In theory the adjudicator will not be affected by the choice of play except in so far as it is suitable or unsuitable for the company performing it, but it must be very difficult for him not to be at least slightly influenced in favour of a group presenting a well-written, challenging play. Of course, well-written, challenging plays turn up frequently in festivals, and if you choose one which he knows very well, although he will probably not be bored by it, you may run the risk that, however hard he tries to keep an open mind, he has very set ideas on how it should be done.

Finances

It costs quite a lot of money to go in for festivals. There is usually a modest entrance fee, but additionally you have to pay the royalty on the play (the festival organizer will want to see that you have a valid licence for the performance), and there may be costumes or props or other equipment which you have to hire. The biggest problem is often the transport of scenery and furniture, and though it is sometimes possible to borrow a van at little or no cost from a friendly local trader, this item may present you with a big bill.

Some festivals offer all entrants a grant towards their costs, but these vary from token payments to more generous sums, and you will need to find out in advance how much money, if any, you will get. Many festivals give competing teams some form of rebate on the tickets they sell, which seems a very fair way of providing a subsidy, and a real incentive to bring supporters in large numbers. Certain festivals give cash prizes to the winners, which is fine if you are among them.

Insurance is usually carried by the festival to cover accidents or losses to the competing teams, but it is as well to check on this, and to cover yourselves additionally if necessary.

16

Other Types of Play and Production

One-Act Plays

The problems in presenting a one-act play are really no different from those of a full-length production, except that there is less time to establish characters and situations, and a greater intensity must therefore be brought to all that you do. For this reason the one-act play may be considered more demanding, but many amateur companies use one-acters as a kind of training ground for new directors and actors, and if you have a largish society you might think of putting on a production of three or four short plays instead of a full-length drama. This will enable you to give a large number of actors a chance (which will probably be good for ticket sales), but you may have to find a different set of stage staff for each play, and may also need more than one rehearsal venue so that the plays can be rehearsed simultaneously.

All-Women Plays

It is not always easy to find suitable plays for an all-women cast, and the difficulty is increased by the fact that the members of all-women groups, such as Townswomen's Guilds and Women's Institutes, are often made up almost exclusively of ladies a little past the first flush of youth, and all too often the attractive plays contain one or more teen-age or early twenties character, which can be an almost insuperable hurdle.

Generally speaking, it is unwise for an all-women group to attempt a mixed cast play (I remember a splendid Viking warrior in an all-women production—five feet nothing, a rather large chest, and a soprano voice emerging from an extremely false-looking set of whiskers), but if you are fortunate enough to have a director of genius, nothing is barred. For many years Mrs Greta Raikes directed the drama section of the South Norwood Afternoon Townswomen's Guild in a series of festival-winning productions of mixed-cast plays, including Shakespeare. She would agree that she was greatly helped by having a number of highly talented actresses, including some who could, without strain, use the lower register of their voices, but the real credit was hers. Even more than with a mixed cast, the director of an all-women production must try to ensure that there is a good variety of voices.

Children's Plays

Children are often sheer delight on the stage, especially the very young ones who, overcome by the occasion, forget all that their teacher has drummed into them. Having fewer inhibitions than adults, children are often very good mimics and respond well to direction. It is likely, however, that they will require even more tuition in stagecraft than those novices who are more mature, for as we grow older, though we may have little interest in drama, we all acquire some sense of how we appear to other people, and this is of use when it comes to presenting ourselves on the stage. Sometimes children can appear to be too drilled, and it is important to make them understand why they are to perform certain actions or to say their lines in a certain way so that they are not simply aping their director. One thing which may help is to persuade them to improvise, using their usually acute powers of observation, and relating their words and actions in the play as far as possible to their own lives.

Since children do not have the preconceived ideas of adults, they have far less respect for such restrictions as the proscenium stage, the well-shaped play, type-casting, and so on, and this gives great freedom to those directing them.

There are many good plays written specially for children, but it is possible to put on adult plays with a very young cast. You may have some difficulties with make-up (I shall not forget the ten-year-old who told me, 'I'm the Mayor of Paris and I have to look seventy years old'—though in fact such a make-up is much easier than to make a child look like a man or woman of forty), but it is the inner belief in the character rather than the outward appearance which carries conviction, and youngsters who have been helped to a full understanding of their parts can produce performances of stunning maturity.

Religious Plays

There is little to say about religious plays that does not apply to any other kind of production, except that you must try to avoid using specially reverent voices and 'holy' attitudes. Religious plays used almost always to be rather sugary and sentimental, but more recently many playwrights have treated religious themes with a more down-to-earth approach and more rounded characters, and it is worth taking the trouble to find such plays.

If you are performing in a church, you may have a visibility problem, so think about building a temporary stage or at least using rostra.

Improvisations

I have already suggested that if you have the time it is worth making the actors in a play improvise what has happened before the curtain rises or what happens to them when they are off the stage. Improvisation is a very useful exercise for actors. It can also be made into an entertainment, for you can improvise your own play. The one essential is a director who has a sense of play construction and of story-telling.

Get your group together, ask them to choose a basic theme, and to select characters for themselves. One or two will probably respond, after which you can either give them a starting situation or allow them to suggest one. Then simply ask them to improvise dialogue and action. Once they have got over a certain shyness, they will begin to act and react, and with any luck the beginnings of a story will emerge. This will often suggest other characters, who can join in. The director's job now is less to carry out his usual functions (which will come later), than to edit what is going on, to tell the actors when they are becoming repetitive or dull or when their improvised dialogue is leading them away from the desired shape of the play. Think again of those headings: exposition, complication, climax, resolution and conclusion.

You should probably not rehearse an improvisation for too long, or it will lose its spontaneity, but although the lines are never written down and may vary from performance to performance, it is possible to get the play after a few rehearsals to a state in which the participants know exactly what they have to convey and when and how. If you prefer, you can of course formalize the proceedings and in fact write out the parts and then rehearse it as you would a published play.

Mime

Another useful exercise which can also become an entertainment is mime. It is an essential part of certain plays in which scenery and properties all have to be mimed—Thornton Wilder's *Our Town*, for instance, or his *The Happy Journey*. Mime depends on careful observation, and it is surprising how many simple actions that we perform every day are quite difficult to reproduce in mime, simply because we do them normally without thinking about them. Try, for instance, combing your hair without a comb, or brushing your teeth without a toothbrush. Of course, as with any kind of acting, mime has to be carefully controlled and therefore may not be a completely accurate reproduction of the action concerned, but must be edited to appear to the audience to be so. Facial and body expressions become extremely important.

If you are miming scenery and properties do try to ensure that every member of the cast knows exactly where everything is. If the characters have to go through an imaginary door, they must all know its precise position, and the siting and type of door-handle that they have to mime.

Pantomime

Pantomimes can be enormous fun. That is the main trouble—the cast often tends to take rehearsals less seriously than for a straight play, and since a large number is usually involved, perhaps with several beginners, including children, it is essential that the director should make sure that the fun does not get in the way of his attempts to achieve an effective show. In particular, business must be most carefully rehearsed, not forgetting to protect the stage and scenery if you are going to have a slapstick scene with custard pies, or water, or whitewash, or even if you are going to hurl lumps of uncooked pastry about the place.

Since there will be many songs, a good musical director is also needed, and I would suggest that in the early weeks of rehearsal the script and the songs should be tackled on separate occasions. Whether or not you include dancing depends on whether you have a competent choreographer available—if you haven't, it is better to omit it altogether.

Musicals

Most of the remarks about pantomimes apply equally to musicals, though it will probably be essential to include dancing (which can also be rehearsed separately until quite a late stage in the production).

If you are presenting Gilbert and Sullivan you probably need someone who is a dedicated Savoyard to direct the show, for though the operas are out of copyright and you can do what you like with them, most of your audience will expect to see the traditional approach and all the time-honoured movements and business.

Revues

Revues give a great opportunity for amateurs to show off their party pieces, and of course you can include sketches and even a one-act play if you wish. If you have any writers or composers in the group, this is an occasion for them to try their hands. Original material adds interest, but if individual members of the group have no ideas of what they could do, there are plenty of published monologues, sketches and songs which the director could suggest to them.

Working With Other Groups

Many amateur actors belong to more than one society, and

provided they can overcome the problems of divided loyalties, must benefit from the experience of acting with different colleagues and under various directors.

Some groups also combine from time to time to mount a large-scale production of some kind, which can be very enjoyable. Those participating must, however, not be chauvinistic about their own societies and must allow themselves to be welded into a team.

The Round

In recent years theatre-in-the-round has become popular, and it has many attractions for amateurs, especially for those who perform in halls with inadequate stage facilities. In-the-round is usually a misnomer, for the acting area is normally square or oblong, and the presentation is 'round' only in the sense that the audience is seated on all four sides. Since for amateur productions the seating usually has to be on the same level as the players, there are sight problems, but these only become acute if you have more than two or three rows of seats, which is rarely possible in the space available.

Although some dislike it, the majority of amateur actors who have worked in the round seem to enjoy doing so. On the proscenium stage the actors are separated from the audience, and there is an invisible barrier between them which has to be overcome, whereas in the round there is a more direct communication between the actor and the audience. On the other hand, the player inevitably will have his back to some of them, so his projection has to be strong at all times.

Of course, there are many other problems. The first obvious one is that you cannot have scenery—at least, not of the conventional kind—and anything that you put on the stage in the way of furniture or other dressing must be low enough not to obstruct the audience's view. At first this may suggest that comparatively few plays are suitable for the round, but in fact there are virtually none that cannot be successfully performed in this medium.

Never underrate the audience's willingness to use imagination. I once directed an in-the-round production of *Tobias and the Angel*, without scenery and without props. I introduced a narrator, who appeared before each scene and told the audience what the setting was. The actors were careful to mime the use of the various properties and to make their entrances and exits as though through doorways. I did use rostra to give some variety to the spectacle, and when one actor had to remain standing on a rostrum for a long period, I placed it by one of the entrances (there are usually four entrances in the round—one at each corner of the square or oblong) where he would not be in the audience's way. Many of the spectators said afterwards that they felt as though they had been participating in the play themselves, and some even told me that they could have done without the narrator's introduction and would have been able to 'see' the scenes without being told about them.

Let me emphasize again that nothing must be allowed to block the view of any part of the audience for more than a short period, and that includes actors standing in one place. If you have to have a large piece of furniture or an immobile actor, at least place it or him in a corner.

If an actor does not move, he not only obstructs the audience, but many of them will not be able to see his face, and the director has therefore to devise reasons for movement, which can be his biggest headache. As a general rule, no stage movement should be made without purpose, but I think a tiny amount of licence in this respect can be taken for the round, though the director must avoid such constant movement that the production seems 'busy'. He will have much more difficulty in focusing the audience's attention where he wants it, so in general the old rule applies that only the character whose scene it is should be allowed to move, and if you have to change the position of characters of lesser importance, you must do so when their movements will not distract the audience's attention from vital lines of dialogue or other actions. Though far from insuperable, the problem is compounded by the fact that an audience takes in only one thing at a time, and any confusion of interest becomes particularly difficult for them when, instead of looking straight ahead at the proscenium stage which is some distance away, they have to use much more eye movement and at times have to turn their heads to follow all that is going on so close to them.

Another difficulty arises with a vital piece of business or prop. Obviously, the actor concerned cannot spin slowly round so that every member of the audience can see it, but it is usually possible to make some alteration in his stance so that at least a majority of them see what is happening.

Make-up for the round needs to be very discreet, even under quite powerful lighting, because of the nearness of the actors to the audience, and this makes it much more difficult, though not impossible, to use character make-ups.

Costumes and properties also present some difficulty. On the proscenium stage it is much easier to get away with tatty costumes and roughly simulated props, but in the round costumes have to be as realistic as possible in quality of material, cleanliness and detail, and props have to be as nearly authentic as you can make them.

It is perfectly possible to present a play in the round simply using the hall's normal lighting, but it is much more satis-factory if you can light the stage area only. There is still bound to be some spill of light on to the audience, but in the main they will be in shadow, and their attention will be focused on the acting area. If they can see the rest of the hall clearly, their eyes may wander to other members of the audience or to actors waiting to make their entrance or indeed to the decoration of the hall. If, however, you can light the acting area intensely, it is extraordinary how unaware the audience becomes of anything except what they see there, and actors can make their entrances, necessarily through part of the audience, virtually unseen until they step on to the stage.

To light an in-the-round production adequately you really need a large number of lanterns of various types suspended from metal bars which themselves are suspended by wires or strong rope from the ceiling. The large number of spotlights is needed because they have to be aimed fairly steeply down-wards (otherwise they will shine into the eyes of the audience seated on the opposite side of the acting area) and therefore each one will cover a limited part of the stage only. By setting the lanterns at various angles on each side of the square or oblong, each one aimed as far as possible across to the other side, you can cover the entire stage area with light. The spots can be fixed to the walls of the hall, especially if it is a small one, but you will run a greater risk of dazzling your audience if you do so. If the lamps are separately controlled, you can achieve considerable variety in the lighting, but it may be difficult or impossible to change the colour of the jellies during the performance, and that is another reason for having a large number of lanterns, so that you can keep some of them in reserve for special effects. The best place for the lighting and sound controls, incidentally, is on the stage of the hall, or in its balcony if it has one.

Apart from the first scene, which can be ready before the audience comes in, any setting of the stage has to be done in full view. Most spectators seem to look upon it as an extra entertainment. Occasionally there may be something which should be concealed so that it is not visible until the action starts, and if so, it could be set under a cloth which is removed during the blackout which precedes the scene, or can perhaps be brought on by one of the actors entering during that blackout.

As has already been suggested by the comments on make-up, costumes and props, the actor in the round is under closer scrutiny than he would be on the proscenium stage. Lack of confidence, uncertainty of lines, and any other such weaknesses will be more apparent. He needs to be very careful about his eye focus, and must always keep his thoughts and his eyes firmly within the acting area.

He must time his entrances very carefully, allowing exactly long enough to walk through the gap in the audience which leads to the acting area and arrive there at the right moment. If he is to be discovered on stage when the lights go out, he has to negotiate that passage in the blackout and then be prepared for the brightness as the lights go up. Fortunately there is usually enough of a glimmer from exit signs and other dim lights for him to find his way.

I should like to suggest that you try in the round to do without a prompter and let the actors struggle out of any difficulty they get into, but if you do not have enough confidence for this, the prompter can be seated among the audience (reserve a seat for her). A prompt which comes from the audience is, however, more distracting and destroys the illusion to a greater extent than one which comes from behind the scenes in a proscenium production.

A variation on the round is the thrust stage, with the audience seated on three sides of the acting area. In this case it is possible to have some scenery and even rear wings. It is easier to arrange movements and there are fewer difficulties with the placing of furniture and the disposal of lighting, but many of the problems of the round remain.

Although it may seem that productions in the round or on a thrust stage are beset with obstacles for the director, the actor, and indeed all concerned, in fact it is a matter less of having more problems, than of different ones from those of the proscenium stage. And the round really can be great fun and very stimulating.

Open Air Productions

Plays performed in the open air differ from other productions only in that so often it rains. You must decide in advance whether the performance will be cancelled and possibly repeated at a later date, or whether you will hastily remove yourselves and your audience to a convenient and available hall. You also have the hazard of passing aircraft and nearby lawnmowers, and in any case, since acoustics are often difficult, you need to make sure that all your actors are aware of the need to be more than usually audible.

Touring Productions

The majority of amateurs perform their plays only in their own hall, or perhaps sometimes in festivals, but there are many other opportunities for giving a show if you are interested. Prisons, old peoples' homes, homes for incurables and the like will often be delighted to have an amateur company come along to entertain, though you may need to give considerable advance warning of your availability. You can also arrange tours, or perform on village greens or in pubs. In such cases you will want to have as little scenery as possible, for ease of transport, and you must be prepared to act on stages of varying sizes, with little or no lighting and often no wing space (take a couple of screens along if you can).

17

Other Activities

Unless you have a large programme of productions every year, there are likely to be long periods when the society is not functioning at all, and the gaps may seem even longer to those who are not involved in one of the productions that you do put on (though it is always possible to find jobs for those who are not in the cast or in the regular backstage team). So how do you keep your membership interested?

There are many things that an amateur dramatic society can do apart from putting on plays. They nearly all demand a certain amount of organization, but the human race seems to contain a number of people who enjoy arranging events for the benefit of their fellows, and you will be unlucky and unusual if your group does not have one of them. These events may also require financing, but provided that you can get a reasonable attendance, a comparatively small entrance fee or a raffle will probably cover your expenses.

Lectures and Demonstrations

It is possible to arrange for professionals to visit you to give lectures and demonstrations on such subjects as make-up and lighting, or you can hire the services of a teacher of drama to spend an evening with you in improvisation or the rehearsal of a scene from a play, or simply in talking about drama. For that matter, of course, you can hire a professional to direct your play, if you can afford it, and you will undoubtedly gain a great deal from his tuition. You may also have among your members people of sufficient experience who would be willing to give lectures or demonstrations or to run some kind of theatrically educational event for you.

Playreadings

Playreadings are often very enjoyable, but you do need to have someone firmly in charge, who will obtain the necessary copies of the play, and allocate the parts at the reading. It is usually a good idea to change the parts around periodically, so that everyone present can have a go, and it is a good opportunity for giving the less experienced members of the group a chance to show what they can do and for allowing others to read parts which might be outside their normal range. Of course, since most people present are likely to be unfamiliar with what they are reading, you will not get a great performance of the play, but an alternative method which should make a playreading more entertaining is to rehearse it first, possibly even adding in simple moves, costumes, properties, lighting and effects.

It is best if the person organizing the playreading has done a little homework first, so that he knows the play fairly well, and can be sure before embarking on each act or scene that each part in it has been allocated to a reader, and can decide when to make a change of readers. He may also have to read some of the stage directions, so that those without copies will know what is happening, but obviously does not need to include directions which are no more than insignificant moves.

Remember that plays are often in copyright, and it may be necessary to pay a royalty for a playreading, especially if you have an audience present. The publisher of the play will advise you.

Other Events

You might consider putting on a 'Summer Night's Diversion', such as my own society did several times. We were fortunate in having available a large lawn and a hall nearby to which we could move if it rained. In one corner of the lawn an actor might be performing monologues; in another a couple would be giving the tea scene between Gwendolen and Cecily from *The Importance of Being Earnest*; in a third corner a group was playing Act V of *The Merchant of Venice*; in the fourth corner two people were reading from a foreign language phrase book as though it were a mini-play written by a demented dramatist; and in the adjacent hall a very brief melodrama was performed on the stage. Each item was timed to last not more than fifteen minutes, and were all presented simultaneously. The audience, having paid for admission, could wander and choose which of the diversions to watch. Having seen one item, they could move to another location to watch the next performance there, and so on, each show being given four or five times during the evening.

Another society honoured its president recently by giving her a sort of 'This is Your Life' evening, in which she recalled her career in amateur drama, with a number of interesting and amusing anecdotes. When she spoke of certain plays of which she had especially vivid memories, brief rehearsed extracts from them were read by members of the group.

If your society has a particularly versatile and talented actor, you might consider allowing him to put on a one-man show, or perhaps he could join with someone else for a two-hander evening.

For any of these or similar activities it is worth appointing a director who will control them with a critical eye and stop them from becoming self-indulgent.

Parties

Parties of all kinds are often popular, especially when husbands, wives and other attachments are welcomed. The best are those which have some theatrical connection, or which include an entertainment of an informal kind given by some of the members. If you prefer a plain cheese and wine party at which people just mingle and talk, that is up to you, but even the most sophisticated and intellectual of amateurs seem occasionally to enjoy letting their hair down and playing silly games involving mime, or charades, or quizzes about the theatre. Or you might like to try a Victorian evening, to which everyone is invited to come in costume.

Many groups have an After-the-Show party. If you do not have to strike the set and clear up the hall immediately after the last performance, you can hold it there and then. Ask everyone to bring something to eat and drink and pool it, so that no single person has the burden of catering. Or you may like to hold such a party a week or so later and combine it with a criticism evening, having asked someone, perhaps from another local drama group, to attend the play and to be prepared to come along and comment on it. The subsequent discussions will be, one hopes, friendly.

Theatre Outings

The live theatre needs support, quite apart from the fact that amateurs can learn so much from the professionals, and theatre outings can be arranged. One London company that I know has a regular outing in late summer to the South Coast. The coach journeys to and from the seaside are taken up with quizzes and word games, all with a theatrical background, the afternoon is spent on the beach, tea is taken in a local cafe, and in the evening the whole group goes to the nearby theatre, benefiting from the party rates which are available if you can get sufficient numbers.

Meeting Other Amateurs

Amateur groups have a tendency to keep themselves to themselves, which is a pity. They don't even attend each other's shows as often as they should, though that is often because the performances coincide with their own or with the later stages of their rehearsals. However, if you establish contact with other companies you may find that you can share many activities together (theatre visits, for instance), and you may make many friends.

One of the most important reasons for getting on good terms with other amateur groups in your locality is that you may be able to borrow scenery, costumes, props and even actors from them, and equally be able to help them out on occasion.

Drama Associations

If there are sufficient amateur groups in your vicinity and there is no local drama association, you might consider starting one. The Norbury and Thornton Heath Drama Association, of which I have the honour to be president, was formed with the main aims of building a little theatre for amateur use and of avoiding a clash of dates for the plays performed by local groups. Both objects proved impossible to achieve, but the association has been vigorously alive for over thirty years and has brought many benefits to its member societies. It runs a very successful annual one-act festival, it owns a considerable amount of equipment which it loans to member groups at very competitive rates, it organizes lectures and demonstrations, it holds various social functions, it produces a newsletter, it provides a criticism service, it has a library of plays, and so on.

Newsletters

Since many drama groups come together only when plays are being produced, it is worth the trouble of producing a newsletter. It does not have to appear with strict regularity, but it is a way of keeping your members in touch with what is going on.

Photographs and Scrap-books

If the society and its members, particularly those in the cast of a production, like to keep a record of your plays, you may want to arrange for a photo-call each time you have a new show. Whether you employ a professional to take the photos or a member of your group who is keen on photography, is up to you, as is the question of whether the photos should be taken during a dress rehearsal (not during a performance, unless it can be done without even the click of the shutter to disturb the audience) or whether you will pose the photographs during a special photo-call. The advantage of the former method is the natural look of the picture, while the second approach enables you to ensure that every member of the cast appears in at least one photo and that you record the most dramatic or funny moments. You may of course use a combination of both ideas.

If the photographs are taken prior to the first performance, the proofs will be ready, with any luck, before the last night of the play, and if possible you should collect orders and the money there and then.

Sometimes the photographer is willing to give the complete set of proofs to the society, and these can be kept not only as a record but also for use as display material during future productions. Try to persuade one member of your group to be permanently in charge of photographs.

Many societies keep a scrap-book. This will contain a copy of the programme for each show, photographs, Press reviews, and anything else that you want to record.

A Word of Warning

Do make sure that your membership is interested in the other activities you think of organizing before embarking on a programme which will involve the committee in a lot of work in the preparation of events which will end up being attended only by the committee members (and only by them out of a sense of duty). Many societies are made up almost entirely of members whose sole interest is in actually taking part in a production, or who are too busy to do more than that.

18

A Final Word

I have tried to show in this book that although putting on a play is a difficult and highly complex business, it can be done without a great deal of experience and without all the facilities of a professional theatre. You may feel that I have still been too demanding. For instance, you may have greeted with a hollow laugh my suggestion that a production needs a large team of backstage helpers, and I am well aware that in many groups the director is also the producer and the stage manager, and that many other functions have perforce to be carried out by members of the cast.

But perhaps the most important failing of what I have written is that I have not made enough of the fact that amateurs put on a play for the pleasure of doing so. I believe that amateur drama is something that you should undertake seriously, working hard at it, trying to learn all the time, and presenting as professional a show in every respect as you possibly can. At the same time no one, especially the director, should forget that it should be fun.

There is an old joke which runs: 'Why do these people do this?' 'For charity.' 'But ought not charity to begin at home?' 'I believe it should.' 'Well, then, why don't they act at home?' If you ask an audience to pay to see your production, or even if you let them in free, you owe them something—it is your duty to entertain them, and to avoid embarrassing them. You are more likely to succeed in this if you enjoy what you do, though it must be the enjoyment which comes from performing to the best of your ability, rather than mere self-indulgence.

It is of course the actor who gets the most obvious rewards. There is great delight to be had in stirring your audience to tears or laughter, to have their rapt attention as they watch and listen to you, to hear their enthusiastic applause as you exit or at the final curtain. Nevertheless, if you are part of the back-stage staff, you should be able to take equal pleasure and pride in your part in mounting a well organized production, and in the friendship of your colleagues in the society.

So the final message is: enjoy yourself! have fun! and break a leg!

Recommended Reading

The Complete Play Production Handbook by Carl Allensworth, Hale, 1976
Produce Your Play by Louis Lentin, Ward River Press, 1982
The Play Produced by John Fernald, Kenyon-Deane, 1969
An Actor Prepares by Konstantin Stanislavsky, Eyre Methuen, 1980
About Acting by Peter Barkworth, Secker & Warburg, 1980
The Craft of Comedy by Athene Seyler & Stephen Haggard, Garnet Miller, 1974
Stage Design by Kenneth Rowell, Studio Vista, 1968
Designing and Making Stage Scenery by Michael Warre, Studio Vista, 1966
Stage Lighting by Richard Pilbrow, Studio Vista, 1971
Stage Sound by David Collison, Studio Vista, 1976
Designing and Making Stage Costumes by Motley, Studio Vista, 1964
Historical Costumes of England from the Eleventh to the Twentieth Century by Nancy Bradfield, Harrap, 1970
Practical Stage Make-up by Philippe Perrottet, Studio Vista, 1975
Theatre Props by Motley, Studio Vista, 1975
The Penguin Dictionary of the Theatre by John Russell Taylor, Penguin Books, 1970
The Art of Coarse Acting by Michael Green, Hutchinson, 1964
Theatre Directory, published in regularly revised editions by Stacey Publications, 1 Hawthorndene Road, Hayes, Bromley, Kent, is an extremely comprehensive and helpful list of theatrical suppliers and organizations. Stacey Publications also publish the splendid, indispensable monthly magazine, *Amateur Stage*.

Index